Mama Said There'd Be Days Like This

(but she never said
just how many)

DØØ62365

Mama Said There'd Be Days Like This

(but she never said just how many)

CHARLENE ANN BAUMBICH

CARMEL • NEW YORK 10512

This Guideposts edition published by special
arrangement with Servant Publications.

Parts of this book have been adapted from articles that first
appeared in various publications including *Marriage Partnership*,
published by Christianity Today, Inc.

Printed in the United States of America
ISBN 0-89283-918-X

Library of Congress Cataloging-in-Publication Data

Baumbich, Charlene Ann
  Mama said there'd be days like this : but she never mentioned
just how many / Charlene Ann Baumbich.
    p. cm.
  ISBN 0-89283-918-X
  1. Baumbich, Charlene Ann, 1945-   . 2. Christian biogra-
phy—United States.   3. Christian life—Anecdotes.   4. Christian
life—Humor.   5. American wit and humor.   I. Title.
BR1725.B357A3   1996
242—dc20   95-4119
                                                                    CIP

Contents

Acknowledgments

Thanks to:

Everyone who reads this book (Days of Risk-Taking);

Beth Feia and Ann Spangler who shared tea with me while perusing possibilities (Days of Dreaming);

Al and Barb Unger who gave me the keys to their lake home, thereby enabling me to meet my deadline (almost) while also getting a respite from Wonderdog Butch who couldn't seem to stop barking while I was trying to concentrate (Days of Hollering Shut-Up! replaced by Days of Wondrous Silence);

Jay at the old Lefty's who made the meanest Veggie Burger and Chili-Cheese Fries I ever tasted (Days of Pigging Out);

Larry Turner for permission to use his poem, *The Bed* (Days of Talented Resources);

My friends and family who let me tell their stories and use their REAL names: Kristen, Jo, Darcy, Marlene, Mickey, Kim, Kathy, Carol, Dad, Wendy, Mary Beth—and to others I alluded to (Days of Thankfulness for the Blessings of Friendships);

Liz Heaney, my editor, who endured dozens of "days like this"—THAT ALL TOOK PLACE WHILE I WAS WORKING ON THIS BOOK, thereby causing me to become hysterical and cry;

Bret and Brian, my grown-men babies who love me, even during attacks of the Big M (Days of God's Grace—meaning the gift of my children, not menopause);

George, my husband, who steadfastly holds down the fort during The Days of Book Writing and all the days in between. I love you, even on days when I don't act like it.

Before I Begin
(really, In the Beginning)

Recently a neighbor asked me how the book was going, and I was excited to tell her that it had officially been titled.

"Great. What?"

"*Mama Said There'd Be Days Like This, But She Never Said Just How Many,*" I said, convinced not only about the accuracy of that statement, but how I believe it to be a divine summation of the contents. Good, bad, and dubious days. Days that are slices of pure grace, and others that make you want to hurl your cookies from the frustration of it all.

I hope this collection of days brings some of your own escapades to mind and helps you to laugh at them as I have done. Or to relish the reminder of that certain Someone you need to remember and hold close—as close as a child nuzzles that favorite blankie to his face.

The days I've written about are as current as yesterday, or as long ago as my childhood. They are days I treasure, and days I buried like a dog buries a bone, only to dig them up and share them with you.

I hope the collective message of my stories infuses your soul with these truths: Every day is a gift, whether we see it that way at the time or not. Every day offers a chance to giggle and backslap, belly laugh and hug, cry and dream, love and forgive. And every day can deliver moments of exasperation so traumatic, all you want to do is catch a slow boat to La-La Land and wave goodbye to your significant others.

Not long after I told my neighbor the title of this book, she called. I was the target of both her barrels. It had been a terrible twenty-four hours, she said. She'd spilled something down her favorite dress and become stranded on the highway and....

"I wish you'd never told me your title, because all I kept thinking was, 'Mama said there'd be days like this.'"

Exactly. And Amen.

1 Discovery Zone

George and I were engaged in lively conversation when he stopped talking for a moment and retrieved his white, no-frills hanky out of his back pocket. Unfolding it, he vigorously blew his nose. I continued to talk without skipping a beat.

After several good snorts, he folded the hanky right on the creases, again and again, until it was returned to its perfect square. He put it in his right hand and slid it down into his back pocket.

When he looked up at me, I had become mute. My mouth was agape. I couldn't believe what I was seeing, and it showed on my face.

"Is something wrong?"

"Do you *always* fold your hanky like that after you blow your nose?"

"Yes. Is that a problem?"

"Maybe."

"Why?"

"After twenty-five years of married life, I had no idea you

folded your hanky back up like that after blowing your nose."

"So?"

"So, I'm sorry to tell you that when I'm doing laundry and find the hanky so neatly folded in your back pocket, I assume it hasn't been used and I simply put it back in your drawer without washing it."

It was George's turn to stand with his mouth agape. After a couple beats passed, he responded.

"No wonder I always have so much trouble getting my glasses clean."

2 When Your Trolley Slips Off the Track

I was sitting in a restaurant, trying to find a polite way to expel the back of my broken tooth from my mouth. It was much worse than trying to get rid of gum because your tongue simply *must* search the vacant spot to see just how big the hole is, while at the same time trying to move the broken piece forward for expulsion.

Two days later (first available appointment, and one day before vacation), I sat in the dentist's chair waiting for repairs. It was the beginning of one of *those* days that never seems to end.

Six Novocaine shots later, my head was numb, but the tooth was not. Since the dentist had to remove the large filling and screw pins down into the tooth to make a foundation for the new filling, he told me it was not a good idea to proceed. Thank you very much.

Drooling, I left the dentist with only ten minutes to spare

before my nail appointment. And you don't cancel your nail appointment when you're leaving on vacation. That procedure, thankfully, went fine.

As I was walking to my car, which was parked across the street from my church, I thought I saw our pastor on top of a ladder. In my attempt to identify him, I stepped in a hole in the grassy area between the sidewalk and the curb. Down I went, off the curb and into the street between the front of my car and the rear of the car parked in front of me.

At first I thought I'd damaged my ankle. The pain bit into my brain, and I laid on the street, taking stock of my condition. I was glad I hadn't knocked myself out, because I was hidden between the cars.

Finally I decided I could gingerly upright myself and get in the car. As I reached for the door handle, I noticed—OH NO!—that one nail was broken way down to the quick, and the polish was ruined on another.

I gimped my way back to the beauty shop, holding my tragic hand in the air and looking quite disheveled. They couldn't believe what had happened in such a short amount of time, nor could they fix me for two hours. Of course I said I'd return.

When I arrived home to cram some work into that time space, along with last-minute laundry and packing, I couldn't find my glasses, and I needed to sew the crotch of George's favorite black polyester pants. (I'm withholding any further comment here.) I found one of those needle threader things with the big eye, set up my machine and began sewing.

Lickety split, I had sewn a big pucker in his pants. And I didn't just sew it, I'd run the needle back and forth a couple times to make sure the seam would hold.

There was no undoing that mess. If I used the seam ripper, I'd be ripping the polyester—and without my glasses, who knows what I might have done, perhaps ruined the pants. (What a shame *that* would have been.) I neatly folded the pants over the kitchen chair and headed for town with only twenty minutes left before my re-appointment. Fortunately, the Novocaine was finally wearing off; unfortunately, the pain from all the injections was throbbing.

One block from the beauty shop, I had a vision about my glasses: I saw myself there in the mirror, glasses atop my head. I parked where I'd parked before to see if I might have lost them during the spill.

There they were, right in the street. Smashed. Someone had run over them... probably me!

That night I phoned my sons, Bret and Brian, to tell them goodbye before our trip. I couldn't help but share my day. By the time I told Bret every last detail he and I were laughing so hard we nearly wet our pants.

"Oh, Mom. Thanks! I needed that. My day was terrible, but yours was worse. I feel better now."

Sometimes we just need a good dose of perspective. And who doesn't feel better after a hearty, grace-filled laugh?

3 The Upchuck That Saved Our Marriage

A miracle has taken place on Second Street, where George and I live. In fact, it is parked in our driveway. Perhaps the new car itself isn't the miracle; but rather, the fact that George and I are still together.

You would think that by now we would have learned how to accommodate each other's polarized philosophies concerning major purchases. But instead, we have learned to gear up for the battle that will swallow us alive until the sales receipt is in our hands, thus disgorging us from the belly of the whale.

You see, George is a firm believer of easing into things, especially new cars. His shopping cycle goes something like this: read, explore, talk, compare, drive. Repeat. Notice the word *buy* is not in this cycle.

I, on the other hand, say "Let's go buy a car—today."

And so, as the time to make a major purchase draws near,

we begin by talking sweetly to each other, hoping that kind words and attitudes will ward off any similarities to past experiences. Which, of course, they do not.

Nevertheless, we cheerfully begin Phase One by independently browsing. George eyeballs a couple of makes on his way home from work; I venture behind-the-wheel a few times in showrooms during my daily outings. George picks up a couple of brochures; I form a few aesthetic opinions. We discuss our findings over dinner.

Already we don't agree. But in our unending quest to maintain peace, we cheerfully decide to give the other guy's favorite another look. Yuck.

This moves us directly to Phase Two: an exhausting search for possibilities. Evenings are spent prowling through lots, crawling in and out of cars that salesmen insist are just what we're looking for. Price tags continue to astound us. We play with the notion of keeping our old vehicle—until it coughs and sputters its death rattle, reminding us why we began this venture.

Finally, we enter Phase Three: I fall in love with a new model. It fits me like a glove. It has power everything. It has a moon roof, which is even better than a sun roof. It has a cool console with the gear do-jobby on the floor. It has leather seats and a four-speaker stereo system. Although I may be sitting perfectly still on the showroom floor, my mind is speeding us down the highway on a romantic weekend getaway.

Then I look at George and am slam-dunked into Phase Four: He doesn't fit in any car that fits me like a glove. He points to the top of his head, drawing my attention to the static electricity that has sucked his hair up to the bottom side of the moon roof. He thumps the side of his foot against the console to emphasize that consoles take up valuable space he needs for his size thirteen shoes. He thinks talk radio programs are as good as audio bliss gets, so why do we need all those speakers? He says the engine is too small and babbles something about gear-ratio something or other. Our faces start to lose their patient grins.

Off to another dealer where Phase Five commences: George finds his dream car. It has loads of space and not a lot of extras. It has digital nothing. It's the worst color ever conceived by a human. Its ratios or whatever are all in order. It is the quintessential Old Geezer's car.

Which leads us to Phase Six: *What am I doing married to this person?* And our relentless pursuit continues.

Eventually, Phase Seven finds a place in our lives: a car we can both live with and perhaps even enjoy. It is a short-lived moment of bliss, however, because as we enter the salesperson's office Phase Eight opens its jaws: the Sticker Price.

Thus begins the true test of our "for-better-or-worse" vows. We hold our breath, hoping the test-driver is actually able to return in our trade-in. Finally the driver reappears in the cubicle and shakes his head as he hands the keys to our salesman. It's downhill from there.

He names a price. We laugh. He asks us what we had in mind. We tell him and he laughs. Runs are made to and from a hidden manager. George and I squabble about what we each believe is a fair price to pay. I want this over so the rest of our lives can resume; George isn't making a deal until every deliberate step is taken during this car-buying dance.

Many people actually end up buying a car at this point. We don't. After five hours, *five hours,* we leave to find a "better deal." Phase Nine gulps us down: hostility. With car dealers, with one another. Why do we have to play this game?

About the time I announce I just can't take it any more, George remembers yet another dealer we haven't tried. He'll check it out tomorrow on his way home, he says.

They have what we're looking for. We meet with the salesman that very evening and repeat our let's-try-to-buy-a-car scenario. After much bantering, this guy's best-deal price turns out to be higher than the last one. We drive home in our rattletrap, which suddenly feels conspicuously like a digestive tract.

George remembers still another place we haven't been. We decide we will browse the lot the next day, which is Sunday, when they're not open.

Eureka! "Car No. 2299" it says in bold black letters on a sticker in the window. I spring a new plan on George.

"How about this? Let's decide what we're willing to pay. You go to work tomorrow and I'll come here first thing in the morning with the checkbook. I'll hand them the keys to our car for a test drive while I tell them which car we want to buy. I'll offer to write the check if the price is right. I promise, George, I won't pay a penny more than we agree. What do you say?"

"Promise? You won't pay a penny more?"

"Promise."

"Deal."

At the crack of 9 A.M. I hand the salesman my keys and explain my plan. As he gives my keys to the test driver, he takes down some pertinent information. My heart thumps. The salesman gives me a price that's worse than the last one. I explain I'm disappointed. He asks me what price I had in mind. I tell him. He says, "If I can get you that price, you'll write the check?"

"Yes," I tell him.

He disappears and returns with the head honcho, whose fingers begin to tap dance on the calculator. He writes down a few things, then quotes me a price that is $91.28 higher than George's and my price.

"This is the best I can do," he says. "I can't even get rid of that twenty-eight cents."

I feel like I'm in a meat grinder. "Is my marriage worth $91.28?" I silently ask myself.

I ask God to give me strength. I remember saying, "Promise" to George.

What if I left and we didn't buy this car? Could our marriage take one more day of this? Absolutely not! How long could George stay mad? I grab a piece of scrap paper lying on the desk and act like I'm tallying up numbers to give myself time to think. Finally, but not easily, my conscience wins.

I put the checkbook in my purse and say, "I'm sorry you can't do anything about the twenty-eight cents, but it's the ninety-one dollars that has put me past what I'm authorized to spend."

I start to leave. The salesman shakes my hand.

"Deal," he says. "Write the check."

Some may say my shrewd buying tactics saved our marriage. I say the whale belched in the nick of time.

4 How to Be a Dipstick in One Easy Lesson

Occasionally I deliver Meals on Wheels as part of an on-going service project of my Kiwanis group. Upon my arrival one day, Carol, the woman in charge of this much-needed senior assistance, helped me carry the many insulated bags and boxes to my car. While we loaded, Carol grumbled that someone had carelessly erred and caused her a lot of trouble that morning. In fact, she was still running behind and feeling frustrated by it.

Suddenly, and before I could open my mouth to say "Don't close the trunk!", Carol closed the trunk.

"Carol! My keys were in there!"

"I didn't think anyone set their keys in the trunk!"

Well, guess again.

Now it was my turn to grumble—to myself, of course.

Didn't people ask if it was okay to close the trunk? Isn't that just common sense?

"I always put my keys in the trunk when I'm loading it so I know where they are." Now we were both in a hurry, due to errors of other people! Haughtily I said to myself, "Guess we're all human, right Carol?"

After a discussion about what our next step would be—and we tried to keep discussion to a minimum because hot entrees and frozen foods were now locked in my trunk thawing and cooling—we decided that Carol would drive me home. Although I may have lapses of good sense, George and I are clever enough to keep an extra set of car keys on the hook inside the cabinet at home, just in case.

I made a deliberate point of locking my car doors with the auto-door lock button before we left it abandoned in the parking lot to retrieve the keys. After all, and as usual, I had valuable stuff strewn about the interior of my car: expired coupons and sale flyers, empty pop containers and crumpled napkins. I hopped in Carol's car and off we went toward my house. My house that was locked. My house that needed either an electronic garage door opener or a set of keys to enter. And you know where those items were. This didn't occur to ME, however, until we'd entered my driveway.

"Oh no, Carol. I locked my car and the opener was in there! I'll have to call a locksmith!" Now, it was once again Carol's turn to grumble, silently, of course. "Guess we're all human, right Charlene?"

Back to the food center we went. Just as we were about to enter the building to make the phone call, a local police officer marking tires for possible parking violations passed by. God's timely angel, just for us, although it hadn't occurred to me that it was a similar angel who'd left me a parking ticket earlier in the month.

"Could you help me? I locked my keys in the trunk."

"Sure. Just let me finish marking these tires." (I thought I heard a devilish snort.) Soon she returned with a magic tool probably also used by the thieves that break into those can't-break-into-it car doors in about 3.5 seconds.

Thanking her profusely, I grabbed the electric garage door opener. Once again, Carol drove me to my house to get the extra set of car keys. At last, I was ready to go. I could just picture the faces of hungry people trying to pry open their doors in their weakened-from-lack-of-food states as I delivered them melted and lukewarm delicacies.

Here Carol and I were grumbling (which was quickly becoming our natural state) about how we hadn't had much time to visit lately, and God, through our errors, had opened a window of time for us to chat while we fruitlessly drove around town. Isn't that just like God?

Finally, off I went on my route. The people weren't weak and angry; they were concerned and, as usual, very thankful for the meal. I was blessed by their words of encouragement and soon forgot my dipstickedness.

Later that day, I was telling a friend about the comedy of errors. Her reply delivered another smashing blow to my ego, "Don't you have a button inside your car that unlocks the trunk?"

"Yes, but I'd locked my car, remember?"

"But not until you locked it to depart for your house, right?"

Mama said there'd be days like this, but she never said just how many.

5   Is It Real, or Is It Just Mucus?

Fever, cough (deep cough), hurts, listless, then irritable—very, very irritable. All the symptoms of pneumonia, I told myself at 4:40 A.M.

After five hours of trying to find six inches for me in Brian's twin bed, I was a zombie with a racing heart. Each of his coughs seemed to dig a little deeper, and I kept as still as possible, not even exhaling much of the time, so I could hear him breathing—which I was afraid he was going to stop doing at any moment.

I was damp and tacky myself, but not from fever. That vaporized room at 4 A.M. seemed like a steamy, dangerous jungle. I was miserable, but sleeping with Brian seemed safer and easier than getting out of the warmth of my own bed every five minutes to answer his cries.

I groped for his forehead, touching damp sheets, trying to get a corner of the blanket for myself so I wouldn't be the next one with pneumonia.

I had mentioned to George the night before how I "just knew" Brian was getting really sick.

"How can you tell?" he asked.

"Oh, you know," I said with my most dramatic motherly flair, "a mother can see it in her child's eyes. We *know* these things."

After surviving the night, I thought the morning phone lines for appointments would *never* open. I perched myself right next to the wall phone (actually I was leaning against the wall to keep from falling over) and began speed dialing at 7 A.M. They told me to bring him in at eight.

Waiting in pediatrics is as dangerous as standing in the middle of a six lane highway. Every child has glassy eyes and looks contagious. I tried to shield Brian under my armpit, but then worried I was keeping the fever in, so I simply tried to position him as far away from germs as I could. Right. But I was sure if Brian did have pneumonia, his resistance would be low, and he'd probably succumb to every terrible disease to which he was exposed.

Once we were finally called into the room and they asked Brian to take off his shirt, the waiting *really* began. I hated seeing my shivering baby coughing and moaning and staring into space while I waited. And waited.

A nurse came, took his temperature, and asked several questions about his symptoms. I gave her every detail, including every drip of snot. She never made eye contact with either one of us, but wrote everything down. She closed the door behind her when she left, and we could hear Brian's chart—containing his life-and-death symptoms—shuffling back into the rack on the outside of the door.

An interminable amount of time later, we heard the chart

once again scraping against the door. Brian sat up straight and a glimmer of fear crossed his face. Would he need a shot?

Finally the doctor walked in.

"How's Brian today?" the doctor asked while skimming his chart.

Dumb. This doctor is dumb, I told myself. How does he *think* he is? Just look at him!

He asked all the same questions the nurse did. Obviously my evaluation of the doctor was correct; he couldn't even read.

He went through the routine, scoping Brian's eyes and nose, feeling his glands behind his ears, listening to him breathe, then making him cough so he could hear the depths of the rattle.

I sat twisting the strap on my purse, wondering if we'd have to go straight to the hospital and if I had the insurance I.D. card in my wallet.

Finally Dr. Dumb spoke.

"Well, Brian's got a cold."

Hefty clinic bill to find out youngest son has common cold. There should be a Chinese moral in that somewhere.

Believe me, I'm glad it was just a cold. However, I was thinking how much more redeeming it would have been to answer, "I was right, it's zefinolaris, Dear," when George called to check. But to have to say it was just a cold…

I'm incompetent as a mother. No, I'm just behind on sleep. No, I just don't have a medical background. No, I'm paranoid.

No. I was simply wrong, simply human. And I'm sure I'd take the same precautions the next time. My children are too precious to risk.

Well, maybe the sun will shine tomorrow and dry up

Brian's runny nose so I can make that long postponed trip to the grocery store. I've already served the it-must-be-time-to-grocery-shop casserole. Everyone recognizes it by its brownish color which comes from mixing whatever was in the vegetable bin, sprouts and all.

In the meantime, Sniffles and I will watch the raindrops trickle and mingle as they run down the window. And I'll console my tired body and fragile ego with that old saying, "It's better to be safe than sorry." I imagine a mother invented that one.

6   Held Hostage in the Dressing Room

If the sales lady told me one more time that the outfit I was viewing in the three-way mirror was "certainly body-friendly," I was going to rip the velcroed shoulder pads out of the "body-friendly" outfit and politely stuff them in her "access ready" mouth.

On the surface the phrase seemed harmless enough. After all, she was just trying to be polite. It was her way of saying that the black, flowing material covered the mid-life marks of a few too many chips and dips. But after hearing the phrase ten times in three outfits, I had heard it nine times too many. Especially after flipping the "body-friendly" price tag over and realizing that it cost even more than that bottle of anti-aging creme I purchased in a moment of insecurity and financial irresponsibility. And I wasn't about to make that mistake again!

I rehashed the episode with a friend, and we decided that

sales people attend seminars that teach them appropriate and tactful language.

"Forgiving" is another word sales people use to describe an outfit's camouflaging abilities. Yes, there must be workshops on how to plump up a dress while the customer stands in front of the mirror believing she is witnessing a body-shrinking miracle.

You know what I mean. You come out of the dressing room looking drab and lumpy, wearing a sad, hopeless expression, and the sales person, in a flurry of motion, adds yet another set of shoulder pads, rolls or pushes up the sleeves, blouses the material at the waistline, stands the collar up, and, *voila!* You seem to have shrunk.

It perks up my ego for a fraction of a second until I remember, *you were not born with this body-shrinking talent, Charlene. You were simply born with the plump part of it.*

Do you remember the one-piece, straight-up-and-down dress that hangs in your closet like an overcooked rigatoni noodle because that's exactly how it looked on your body once you brought it home—without the sales lady? The miracle worker who whipped into your dressing room armed with a "faaaabulous" belt, a scarf, and a couple tricky ways to tie it? Those perfect accessories you didn't buy because you were sure you had something in your wardrobe bag of tricks that would pull off the same effect.

Wrong. No, I'm not falling into that trap again; I'm going to try on outfits until I find one that sings in a key that comes naturally. Not one where I have to reach falsetto pitches to wear in comfort.

And so I slip into, pull on, tug up and, in general, hurl around the dressing room until I just can't take it any longer, and, once again, come home empty-handed. Or, worse yet, with something that I settle for. Something that the sales person brought me in "another" size, a "more appropriate size in that garment, which is obviously cut on the conservative side." Something I get home and don't like as well as the "body-friendly" number I opted against in a self-righteous huff.

As I sit staring at the new outfit unbagged and draped across the living room couch—noticing the color isn't what it appeared to be under the fluorescent lights in the dressing room—I ponder the possible error in my judgment. Perhaps that annoying sales lady wasn't so bad after all. Maybe I was just in a rotten mood. Maybe I should choke down my pride and take this blah-looking specimen back. Trade it in for the black flowing thing. After all, considering that I've been gaining weight steadily for the last several over-forty years, I don't own that many clothes that fit the way they used to. Appropriate things. Things that are forgiving. Things that are, shall we say, body-friendly.

7 George and Charlene in the Garden of Calories

This is the first time in our marriage that my husband and I have been Chunkos together. Chunkos translated: pudgies, fluffies, middle-aged spreadies.

Although we have each taken numerous turns acquiring the rather unlofty title of Chunko, we have never been so unfortunate as to have found ourselves there together. Our huge box of photographs is a visible reminder of this truth, but, unfortunately, those pictures are in the same state we are: overflowing.

The first episode of the four letter word that starts with "D" and ends with "T" came before we were married. George was eating nothing but boiled eggs, drinking water by the barge-load, and driving throughout the country looking for a little-known commodity called farmer's cheese.

I, on the other hand, had been successful at weight

reduction several years previous by existing solely on carrot sticks and steak. Of course, by today's cholesterol standards, we should both be dead, not thin—and we are neither, at least as of this writing.

As our nuptials approached, I lost more weight and glued on fake fingernails in an attempt to look dreamy in the wedding pictures. Something I probably would have accomplished had it not been for my dorky taste in head pieces and the fact that all but two of my glue-on nails were off for the hand-on-hand photo.

During this same period, George was the first to, ahem, blossom. Truthfully, I think perhaps he'd already started before the vows; probably a slingshot reaction to finally finding the farmer's cheese. Nevertheless, on our wedding day, George was up and I was down when it came to body elasticity.

When we are at our natural weights, which we can no longer remember, we are opposites anyway: George is six-foot, two inches with a large (size thirteen shoe) frame, and I am five-foot, three-and-a-half inches with a medium frame. Okay. Maybe a medium-large frame, but you get the picture.

Somewhere along the line, we started exchanging Chunko-dom status: George shrank and I expanded. This became brutally clear on a fishing trip. I had to wear a pair of his jeans for a half day and they fit! Oh sure, child-bearing had perhaps expanded my hips, but relentless bags of crunchy snacks had turned my thighs tank-size.

Now that I think about it, perhaps that was how we stayed opposites. One got thin because the other was actually consuming every bag and package of junk food in sight; thereby shutting the door to temptation for the other.

Eventually a high blood-sugar scare sobered me into an exchange-list diet. Fear incites self-discipline, I learned. Once again, I shrank... but George mysteriously expanded.

In reality it wasn't a mystery at all. George was always called upon to finish what was left on my plate that didn't fit my diet. I'm telling you, I had amazing control. I didn't even lick frosting off my fingers when baking birthday cakes.

And then my blood-sugar level leveled. And that was the end of denying myself edible goodies. About the time George decided he was going to join me in svelteness, I was no longer motivated by the threat of death.

And so the story goes, and goes, and goes until... here we are, Chunkos together.

One would think that dieting together would make life easier. After all: Misery loves company. If I'm going to be miserable because I blew it and polished off the Cheetos, why shouldn't he be filled with the same guilt? There's always another bag to wave in front of him. And if he has been a bad boy in terms of caloric intake, why shouldn't he buy me Charleston Chew candy bars for a surprise? (Something that told me he loved me even though I was a Chunko—this really delighted me until he suggested that we *share* the chocolate.)

These days, if he tried to finish the leftover food on my plate—which, of course, there never is—I would undoubtedly pierce his hand with my fork. If I suggest he not mound that second helping on his plate, he would undoubtedly stand up—stretching his king-size frame to the max—and dare me to stop him.

The more we think and talk about "having to do something about this," the more we are focused on food. Buttered popcorn. "Want some, hon? I'll make it." Pizza.

"What a day! Let's just call out." Candy. "Better finish this off so it's not here to tempt us."

We have no one to set an inspiring example. We have no reason to feel, "Gee, I shouldn't let myself go since my spouse is in such wonderful shape." We have no shame.

What we have, however, is plenty of chiding. Even though we lure each other into our sinful feasting, we take pleasure in noticing and pointing out the other's shortcomings. Always a good way to ignore self.

"Don't tell me about my double chin," I chastise, "when I have an entire stack of your britches to sew because the crotch ripped out!"

"You're the one who grocery shops and buys this junk," he snaps back.

"So I didn't buy the junk this week and look at you! You're pilfering the dark side of the pantry!"

What we don't say and do blatantly, we find great pleasure and challenge in hiding and seeking. I have become a regular Sherlock Holmes at detecting George's telltale bread crumbs and the peanut butter smears he deposits in the wee hours of the night. And he has discovered my hidden stashes—and takes edible advantage of them, I might add.

In the meantime, we roll our Chunko bodies in front of the television, pig out, and talk about getting serious about "this" tomorrow. All the while, "this" gets bigger.

And so we have to do something about "this."

No. We each have to be accountable for ourselves. After all, we've done it time and again. George and I agree. We should. We must. We owe it to ourselves and each other.

All we have to do is polish off this bag of pretzels, and then we'll be ready. Right, Dear?

8 Giggles and Backslaps

I mmediately following the "and the winners are…" announcement, the girls began to run toward one another, arms outstretched, hurling their bodies into an embrace, clutching, squealing. Then they exchanged partners and the hysteria began again. Kristen was in the middle of it, her pompons abandoned on the floor like giant dust balls.

Jo, Kristen's mother, and I sat side by side on the gymnasium bleachers. Smiling. Clapping. Enjoying. Trying to capture the energy and bottle it for our mid-life selves. Happy that the day-long pompons competition had finally come to an end because our "ends" had lost their cushy bounce.

"You know, boys don't do that," I said.

"What?"

"Squeal," I responded without looking at her. "They grunt and high-five. They strut and look cool. They smack butts. They nod without moving their eyes. They don't squeal."

I knew this first-hand. As mother of two boys, I'd spent

hours seasoning bleacher buns at many a sport, high-school wrestling in particular.

At that moment, every cliché I'd ever heard about the sexes seemed to be well-founded. Although Kristen and Brian were only hours apart in age—Jo and I met in Lamaze classes and ended up delivering on the same day—they were worlds apart in many ways, right from the get-go. One was an overdue pink cherub and the other a two-week early bellowing boy (this should have been our first clue). There Jo and I stood, ogling through nursery windows together.

Birthday number one found Kristen shyly grinning, her five-inch long coal black ponytail bouncing at the back of her head. Brian was practically bald; a few slick hairs crawled toward his eyes.

Brian ran through the house; Kristen struggled, not very successfully, to overcome gravity. Kristen stuck her fragile finger gently in her chocolate frosting and delicately poised the little taster to her tongue; Brian snatched his entire piece claw-like and crammed the crumbling mess into his gaping mouth.

Birthday number two found Kristen reciting the alphabet, forwards and backwards, and whimpering at the slightest reprimand. The dexterous Brian threw and broke things and grinned at screaming, exhausted parents. Kristen's folks were in awe of Brian's physical command; George and I wondered why the alphabet song had produced nothing at our home.

As the birthdays passed, Kristen and Brian's thumb-sucking was respectively replaced with nail polish and war paint, braids and stitches, giggles and backslaps, dolls and forts, and girlfriends and boyfriends.

Then by age sixteen, their natural tendencies grew

stronger and they cultivated new talents, skills, and other inclinations. Kristen not only had pompons and was in all the honors programs, but she was an ace swimmer. Brian not only slew trophies in several sports, but managed to pass into tenth grade. And here we were, sitting in the bleachers, watching them grow into adulthood, wondering what would come next.

Oh sure, not all clichés ring true. I, in fact, didn't fit many of them as a child. I was bald and a tomboy. I loved baseball and hunting. Can't now, couldn't then, spell for beans.

Just the same, I bet I squealed. Whether I wanted to or not, I just bet I did.

9 Fly the Friendly
(but not *too* Friendly)
Skies

Every time George and I get seated on an airplane (which isn't all that often), George starts holding his breath. Not because he's afraid to fly, but because he's afraid I'll strike up a conversation with the person next to me and things will get out of control. Like they did several years ago.

We were on our way to Albuquerque to visit family. George had the window seat—he always gets the window seat—I had the squeeze-play seat, and a nice young woman had the aisle. After getting settled, we listened to the seat belt instructions, rifled through the magazines in the pocket in front of us, and checked for the barf bag. We never need the barf bag, but it's always nice to know you're getting everything you've paid for.

Not long after we were airborne, the nice young lady and I began a light conversation. We were both psyched about vacation, and soon we were on a regular yackety-yack roll. George even chimed in a few times.

As the conversation continued, we touched upon our careers. She worked in a lab; I was a writer. We found one another fascinating and time flew. Before she departed during our stop-over, we exchanged business cards. I told her to give me a call if she ever came through Chicago. We were only about a half-hour from the airport and I loved visiting with people. "You never know," I said, "you might have a couple hours here sometime." If she had quite the layover, I told her, maybe she could even come for dinner. Yackety-yack and she was gone.

Several months later I received a letter. I didn't recognize the name on the return address, but I was curious. Sometimes I receive letters from people who've read my books or heard me speak. (I love that!) Perhaps this was a perk of encouragement.

The letter went something like this. I'll cut to the important parts.

Hi. I'm coming to Chicago around the 4th of July. (Who is this? I ask myself.) *I'll be staying there for several days.* (Is this the woman I met on the airplane?) *Life's been busy at the lab.* (Oh yeah, it is her. It might be fun to get together for lunch or something.) *I'm anxious to see you again.* (Bret's gonna be here over the fourth, too. He might enjoy meeting her. She was pretty cute, as I remember.) *I'll be staying with you.* (WHAT?) *And my sister is coming, too.* (What? What!)

She went on to say how nice of me it had been to extend such a welcome. She continued with flight information. She hoped times were okay. She said she hoped I remembered her.

This was more than squirrely. This was weird. Very weird. What kind of a person meets someone once, then invites herself and a guest to stay at your house for several days?

44

When George arrived home that evening, he set about his usual routine. Bathroom, pick up mail, go to lounge chair, pull up foot rest, read mail.

"Who's this?" he asked, reading aloud the name on the return address.

"Just read it." He began reading the two-page letter out loud, stopping every few lines, asking me the same questions I'd ventured as I'd read the hand-written pages.

"This isn't that woman you met on the plane on the way to Albuquerque, is it?"

"Yes, dear. Keep reading."

"She's coming to Chicago?"

"Yes, dear. Keep reading."

"What? She's staying here?" (pause, pause) "What? She's bringing her sister?!" (pause, pause) There was more he uttered, but it wasn't too hospitable.

The ensuing conversation was very lively. It could have turned into all-out war had it not been that I couldn't decide which side of the argument to dig my trench on. I vacillated between *this will be a fun adventure* and *what kind of person would actually do something like this*? It was a little scary. I did not respond to the letter; we needed time to think this through.

We happened to be having dinner with some friends a couple days later, and of course we couldn't help but begin talking about this strange intrusion to our lives. "What?"

"Did you say she worked for a lab? What kind of lab?" our friends asked. Inside my head a niggling voice of reason raised a chorus of unsettling doubts:

What if she was a psycho?

What if she had a police record?

What if this was a set-up for who knows what?

What if this was simply an opportunity to have a little fun in life?

Finally my own kinder, gentler nature cast the deciding vote:

I let her know I'd received her letter. I told her both my sons would be in for the holiday and that beds would be in short supply. (I think I subconsciously hoped this would dissuade her. I mean *them*.) I worried. I told everyone I knew about our upcoming company so if something happened to us, they'd know who to track down.

In summation: They came, they did Chicago (we all did it together), they went, we were glad they went. The entire episode had its good, bad, and dubious moments, for sure, but we all survived.

The last time we went to Albuquerque and I began a conversation with the person next to me, I heard George sigh. Then I felt a jab in the ribs. When I turned to face him, he raised his eyebrows. I knew just what this secret code meant.

Nevertheless, I conversed with this person. Even gave her a speaker's brochure because she asked for one.

So far, so good. Maybe she'll pass it on and I'll be invited to her hometown for business. Maybe she'll even phone sometime.

Maybe I'll start screening my calls.

10 Hands Across America

I simply had to be a part of it. The idea that people could form a human chain across the entire country by linking hands was irresistible. I couldn't understand why everyone wasn't dropping their everyday life to participate.

I had finally received a confirmation from the official "Hands Across America" people as to where my place in line would be. "Please Report To: Rt. 45 Between Iroquois Mile 7.0 and Mile Marker 6.0, South of Buckley in Iroquois County. Check in Near Mile 6.0, 1 Mile South of Buckley (Exit 272 Off I-57)."

Armored with my official T-shirt, visor and pin, (I sent $35 for the entire works) I was ready to head to Buckley to help make history. My husband said, "Have a good time and be careful. I'll watch for you on TV." My son didn't want to "travel to someplace I never heard of to hold some geek's hand." So be it. I wasn't going to miss perhaps the biggest event in my lifetime, so I set off alone, except for the voices of yackers on the CB.

When I started getting near Route 57, I picked up the

mike and asked a trucker if he had seen any backup. "Negatory." After re-reading the bulletin, I discovered I was still seventy miles from my exit. At this point I ran into a string of buses from Janesville, Wisconsin with "Hands Across America" signs perched in the windows. Waving my visor as I passed, I soon saw another string of buses bulging with sailors.

From this point on, nearly every car, van, pickup, or bus had a similar banner. I stuck my official envelope in the window. I was no longer traveling alone, and the seventy miles passed quickly. Soon I was in Buckley, but not before I saw many vehicles exit at Gilman and heard that several of the buses would be unloading in Paxton, one town past my destination. These would be my links.

I headed for ". . . the policeman down the road who will tell you where to park. There's a big crowd down there already. You can't miss it," so said by a proud local.

"BUCKLEY WELCOMES HANDS ACROSS AMERICA," read the sign. Flags were waving and refreshment stands were lining the main street. A country western band was playing next to the information booth.

I signed in at information and was told to report "one block north by the grocery store twenty minutes prior to countdown." When asked how many were in my party, I responded, "Only me." I spared them any explanation and picked up a paper with words to "We Are The World," "Hands Across America," and "America the Beautiful."

The Buckley Baseball Team, Lions Club, 4-H Club, and Youth Group all had stands set up selling everything from hot dogs to raffle tickets for a picnic table. Buckley Fire and Ambulance was selling hot dogs and pop, with "all proceeds to go to lake improvements and equipment." There were even handmade rag rugs for sale. The sense of community was familiar.

A lady grabbed my arm and said, "I was standing next to you in the information line and heard you say you were by yourself. I'm standing with a group of friends down there (she pointed) you'd sure be welcome to join us." She lived eighteen miles away, but shared the hospitality of everyone I spoke with.

The announcement was made that we were to line up on the west side of the street. At exactly two o'clock the siren would go off and we were to start holding hands and singing. After fifteen minutes, the siren would ring again, signaling the end. A couple shuttles were available for anyone whose spot was a half mile out of town. I headed "one block north by the grocery store."

My heart sank. No one was coming down Route 45 from the north into town. I remembered how many got off at the Gilman exit and wondered how long the gap was between us. As I looked down Route 45 toward the south however, there was no break in people. I hoped the sailors venturing to the exit past Buckley (Paxton) were somewhere down this link.

The line jostled back and forth as each of us tried to get comfortable while either being squashed or stretched to the limits. The siren rang, my heart raced, and the music for "We Are the World" began. At first only a few scattered voices could be heard, but everyone joined in on the chorus and it echoed loud and clear.

Most of us didn't know the words to "Hands across America," but it didn't matter. We weren't there to sing; we were there because we wanted to show the world we cared about the hungry. We were a part of something much bigger than ourselves, our town, even our country.

49

The siren went off in the middle of the song; we ignored its blare. None of us wanted the moment to end and we held hands for some time.

Okay, so we didn't pull off the coast-to-coast human chain. But maybe we should be careful how we define success, even when we are missing a few links.

11 Birth of a Techno Geek

I'm still not sure exactly how it happened. This confession I am soon to make would probably be considered a triumph for many of you. But not me. I vowed and took a very verbal stand against this "thing I did." I was convinced I was incapable of it. I considered it a six-letter dirty word.

My downfall started the day we bought the Color Monitor (CM) for our computer. It was a necessary purchase, not something we did lightly or out of an urgent need to smash to the ground in color while playing Flight Simulator.

In fact, I don't play computer games. They trigger my brain to scream: "You are an uncoordinated ditz who doesn't even recognize the enemy."

So, you see, I only word process. I have never read my DOS book. I don't want to read my DOS book. I do not want to understand computer language. I don't want to get hooked on data bases, whatever they are. I just want to write. And I had been happily doing so, until we bought the CM.

I said it was a necessity. Well it was. We bought a program to help our son prepare for the SAT test. It wouldn't run on our system. Even though it was supposed to work on a monochrome monitor, it wouldn't work on ours.

My friend the computer wizard, explained there were two "cards" in my system; the stupid machine wanted to read off the color card instead of the monochrome one.

It was either buy another program for the SAT test, or get a CM. And since we had four programs people gave us that didn't work on our monochrome monitor, a CM it would be.

Thus arrived the CM in my office. My friend caught me casting sidelong glances at it, and patiently explained things to me, the Computer Illiterate One. All would be well, he assured me. It was a simple matter of plugging things in, he said, and so it was.

First I tested the SAT program. It worked. Then I dug out one of those games just to test the new equipment.

But I couldn't remember what I was supposed to tell the computer at the A prompt, so I called the friend who had given it to us. Step number two in my slide. He wasn't home. However, his wife, who also "does" computers, suggested I try typing EK. No go.

"Get a directory on it," she said.

"How do I do that?" I responded.

"You don't know how to call up a directory?" she asked, her voice rising two octaves.

"No. I have no desire to become a (pause, pause), a (pause, pause) Hacker." I could barely get the word to roll off my lips.

She sighed, then began to walk me through a series of cryptic directions. I read to her what appeared on my screen as we proceeded through the dark back alleys of Computer-land.

"Try this," she said. No go. "Try this... that... now do this... change directories... and on and on and back-slashes... secret codes...."

Suddenly, my computer played a song and a tanker appeared on the screen.

"You did it," she squealed.

I sat staring at a tanker that slowly turned and aimed its giant barrel at me while the music played a triumphant song.

The tanker fired in my face just as my friend squealed in triumph: "You're a Hacker! You Hacked!"

What was I coming to?

12 Juror Number 73

The witness lunged out of her seat screaming, "But she told me so the night before she bought the gun!" Tears hugged her chin and her arms clung to her own slender waist as she crumbled back into her chair.

"People of the jury, this evidence is hearsay and should immediately be stricken from the records and your minds."

Forget? How could I possibly erase the damning evidence that rattled my conscience?

My thoughts spun as I watched the spittooned toothpaste take one last swirl around the edges of the drain before the rush of the water carried it away. Slowly, I stood up and studied myself in the mirror. Was this the face of a woman who could erase such a scene?

"Oh, for Pete's sake. Stop imagining such drama," I watched myself say aloud. "You'll probably get a case involving a compulsive park-in-the-no-parking-zone dolt." I quickly applied extra blush in case the lighting in the courtroom was bad.

My official call to duty had arrived with the Christmas

cards on Christmas Eve. My service period was to begin at 9 A.M. on January 20, one short hour from now. I had probably used 103 local units on my phone bill calling almost everyone I knew to tell them the good news: I was Juror Number 73.

"Take something to read," a friend said. "It is so boring. I've heard about people who sat for five days just waiting and never did get on a case."

"No way," I retorted, practicing my official juror voice. "Our county uses a One Day, One Trial system. If I don't get picked (oh, but please, please I want to) the first day I go, I'm out of there."

"Well, you better take something to read anyway."

I started packing my briefcase. No sense looking like a novice. Files from work, manuscripts to edit for a friend, lots of blank paper, and a book about finding time. Perhaps I would finally have time to learn how to find time, but I hoped not.

A lifelong resident of the area, I knew exactly which parking lot on the east side of the courthouse the form was talking about. I eased into a parking spot at 8:35 A.M. A car pulled up next to me from which a businessman exited, carrying a briefcase.

I smiled at him as I locked my door and pondered the fact that he probably thought I, too, was an attorney, what with my briefcase and all. I decided to act the part of an attorney instead of a lost housewife. I entered the building with a spring in my step and turned to go up the stairs like I knew where I was going. So did the businessman.

Ends up we were both in the jury pool.

The man checked in first and quietly asked, "Where's the little boy's room?" I decided he would be the lenient type when it came to sentencing.

"Juror Number 73 reporting, Ma'am." I was handed an official Juror tag and told to take a seat. The room I chose, the No Smoking Room, was already two-thirds full. From what I could see through the haze in the smoking rooms, they were filled to about the same capacity.

I parked myself on the end of a circa 1950 couch with bumpy cushions. Scanning the room, I noticed some were reading, one lady was knitting, and many were wearing an expression I had seen many times in the primate house at Brookfield Zoo. Eventually nearly 180 jurors filled the official rooms.

"There are twenty million other things I'd rather be doing than sitting here," a female voice behind me griped. A mumbled agreement rumbled through the room. Personally, I was glad for the opportunity to do absolutely nothing but twirl my hair if I chose.

"I had to show up today or be held in contempt of court!" a deep male voice boomed. "The first time I got called I didn't show up. I had a chance to come here or go to Vegas. No choice." Snickers quickly faded. I contemplated the fact a juror could be held in contempt of court.

"I heard there's no restrooms or eating facilities," a voice whispered a little too loudly for a whisper.

"That's why the businesses downtown don't want the courthouse moved to the county complex," a man sitting near the window replied. "They'd lose too much business."

A voice crackled over the PA system, telling us all to be seated in the No Smoking Room for an orientation film. A man issued a few short directives before the Sony was turned on.

"Wear your juror badge with the word 'Juror' facing out." I feared for today's defendants as I held my breath, hoping no one in the room reached for their badge. Did they think we were complete morons?

"Assemble in the hallway next to the vending machines if your number is called."

"Once you are selected for a jury, the judge is the authority, even if what he says conflicts with what you have already been told." Scenes from the Jim Jones tragedy raced through my mind.

We were informed there were seven jury trials scheduled for the day.

We were told not to use any other restrooms besides the ones in our area. We were not to leave the floor, and the courthouse cafeteria was off limits. We could order a cold sandwich that would be delivered to our room at noon, but they were out of roast beef.

The movie was thought-provoking and made me feel a deep sense of responsibility. Perhaps because it reminded me that my fate might someday rest in the hands of people like me. Perhaps it was the dramatic music.

We were told to leave our badges on at all times and warned not to talk to anyone about any cases. And if anyone should try to talk to us about it, we were to tattle right away.

Lights up. It was time to find the "little girl's" room, which soon led me to discover what the entertainment committee dreamed up many a year ago. One bathroom. One stall. Something to do while you wait for your official juror number to be called. Stand in line. Fortunately, the pop machine and free coffee and tea were at your fingertips as you waited in line so you could start the cycle over again after you finally got your turn.

Or, you could whittle away your time standing in line for one of the two telephones, which two individuals, one male with his sleeves rolled up and one female in a very tight brown business suit, had decided were installed solely for their personal use.

If I were the type who liked more action than standing in line and had bookmaker tendencies, I could start taking odds on who would surely explode first while they waited for a phone: the pacer wearing black opaque pantyhose and very large earrings, or the man with the scrunched up face rattling change in his pocket, much to the annoyance of the lynch mob staring at him.

11:10 A.M. No one had been called. Tension was at a peak. Smoke from the smokers room had conquered the entire floor. Many had turned to the magazine rack in desperation. Selections ranged from a Church Music Directory to a magazine advertising a lead story of "How to Make Yourself a More Interesting Person."

The Gestapo at the entrance to our area (disguised as a pleasant-looking receptionist eating a bag of Fritos) barked at a man heading down the stairs, "You cannot leave the floor. Didn't you listen to the directions?" Her shouts slammed shut the mouths of eleven sleeping people who immediately coughed and remembered they were mad.

Noon. The click of the PA system being turned on brought a desperate cry of "Life!"

Three trials would no longer need jurors. We could leave for lunch, and were to be back at 1:30 P.M. Unless we had ordered a sandwich, in which case we were to stay where we were.

Stampede.

I must say lunch was enjoyable. I dined with two new friends I made on the walk to town. We ate at a place that had fortune cookies so we would be assured of receiving encouragement during our lunch break.

1:30 P.M. Lockup again.

"Last time I was called for this we were let out at 1:45 P.M." Cheers.

"Last time I did this, a panel for a jury was called at 3:45 P.M. and selections weren't over until 6 P.M." Groans.

I noticed everyone was less tense than they'd been in the morning. There was more chatter. A table that all morning drew only one solitaire player and three silent observers now bustled with a game of spades. I entertained myself watching a group of strangers team up, bid, and work together toward a win. A lot less stress than playing with one's mate, I mused.

I finally cracked open the book about finding time, which I enjoyed until page 66. Then the author launched into statistical evidence that concluded that by the time we die, billions of brain cells—billions—remain untapped. Seems we only tap into about 10 percent of our capabilities before we check out.

"I can't think of any reason I should have to know that," I found myself saying to a man sitting next to me wearing a plaid shirt.

2:30 P.M. They called the first panel of twenty. I held my breath in anticipation. No luck. Right over me like I wasn't there. They probably knew about my brain cells.

4:00 P.M. Dismissal. Your check will be in the mail. Thanks. Stampede.

Juror Number 73 sighed, picked up her briefcase, and headed for the car. Oh well, this was not motion picture fodder, but at least it spared me from washing ring-around-the-collar for a spell.

13 The Birdman of Second Street

S oon George will disassemble the lawn furniture and put away the porch swing. He will stack everything neatly in the garage, tucking us in for another Illinois winter.

Of course his relentless rearrangement of the basement to accommodate the stuff that doesn't fit in the garage won't produce more space, but it will be a fall chore he can cross off his list. I often chide him about this list, a list not unlike the one he produces for vacations that reads "Socks: brown, black, white, color." (The only *other* color he has is blue.)

A few winters ago, temperatures were stuck sub-zero for days. Outdoor activities were limited to emergencies such as helping neighbors get their vehicles started or making icy-road, death-defying runs to the store for bread, toilet paper, or one of my red licorice attacks.

But there was George, lugging a four-by-eight-foot piece

of plywood to the foot-deep, snow-packed back porch. In and out of the icy winds he went, carrying bird seed and a warm bowl of water to place smack in the middle of the plywood.

I stood in the cozy house drinking tea and watching through the kitchen window, pouting all the while. "For Pete's sake. He gives those birds more attention than he gives *me*," I said to the dog and to George when his task was complete. He didn't want the birds to freeze their fragile feet or die of thirst, he said.

Methodical approaches do have their advantages. I guess people in the tool and die trade need ultra order. But by the time George has drawn a schematic of the wall and disappeared to find a yardstick to target the exact location where the nail should go, I've already given the situation a serious eyeball and hung it.

I picture this scenario the minute he asks "Do you want a fire tonight?" First, he checks to make sure nothing has nested in the chimney. Then he opens the flue, carries up the kindling and arranges it, stuffs endless wads of paper under the grate, positions the logs just so, strikes a match... and warms my soul.

Then there's the annual garden routine. The ten-by thirty-foot plot of earth that he insists will bear tomatoes, green peppers, sprawling cucumbers, and upright rows of green beans, radishes, and onions.

It is a sight to behold. I remember the days when Mom made her furrows for seeds: she walked a straight line dragging a stick in the ground. Not George. He gets out stakes, string, and measuring implements to chart his plan. The draftsman in him simply cannot begin without a precise template.

At the end of a spring Saturday, I can find George wearing dirt, sweat, and a big grin. "Come see the garden," he says, about the spindly plants and patted down lines. And sure enough, little sprouts are making their way via the tender care of this man's large hand that wears a size thirteen ring.

Then I need to see it again after the rabbits have gnawed off half the green beans, which they always do, and George has laboriously planted seeds between the sprouts that escaped the rabbits. In fact, he saves part of the seed pack, folded with a neat crimp in the top to keep the seeds from spilling, just for the replanting.

And while George labors in the garden all summer, leaving a trail of sweat-laden clothes and foul-smelling socks behind him, he fights not only the heat and humidity, but a crabby wife who doesn't do well with high temperatures.

"When are you bringing the fan up, George?" "I hate summer, George!" "George, have you checked the air conditioner?" "George, when was the last time you changed the furnace filters? The house is full of dirt" (The fact that I haven't dusted since, well, never mind, seemed irrelevant at the time.) "I just can't sleep when it's hot, George." "George, can't you at least pick up your socks and get rid of that mess around your chair?"

Then, of course there's the fall fishing agenda. First George digs the worms. Then he packs the car with endless rods, tackle boxes, fishing nets, a boat motor, gas can, and everything else on his list including back issues of *Fishing Facts Magazine*. Mounds of magazines that he refuses to throw away (though they haven't netted us any more fish since his subscription started) but that he reads and feels clever about anyway. "Just in case we fish on a lake that...," he says. "I know one of those magazines has an article about...."

But oddly enough, as annoying as his list-making and

methodical approaches are to me, I find that his quirks occasionally reveal why I love this man.

During his unemployment, when there was too much time and too little money, he pursued list-making with a vengeance and built an office for my budding writing career. A career that at that time consisted of my desire to become a writer. But my desire to become a writer was on his list. Yes, I was on his list.

He takes care of me in his absence. When I am venturing on a trip alone, he always readies the car. Tires checked. Tank topped. CB hooked up for chatty me to pass the time while I travel. Or "Just in case...."

And I recall his gentle thoroughness every morning when I lay in bed and listen as he checks the locks on the doors before he starts his one-and-one-half hour trek to work. Locking the outside world away from his still-slumbering wife. Protecting her.

<u>14</u> It's One of Those Days

It's one of those days when my shoes won't stay tied.
It's one of those days when my gerbil died.
My bike has a flat but it doesn't matter
'cause it snowed.

I needed to talk to my dad but couldn't.
I want to eat chocolate cake but shouldn't.
I found my black patent shoe but it doesn't matter,
'cause I can't find the other one.

I called Grandma to invite her for Thanksgiving dinner.
She said "No, we're just staying home this winter."
I'm lonesome for family but it doesn't matter,
'cause maybe my girlfriend can play.

I phoned her for lunch but she couldn't come.
I hope my phone rings and it's anyone.
I cleaned up my room but it doesn't matter,
'cause I don't like it that way.

Kids all have bad days, everyone knows.
Someone pats them on the head and says,
   "That's how it goes."
But no one is here to tell me that—and it matters,
'cause I'm forty one.

15 Dukes of Hazard, Suburban Style

One night when Brian was six years old, he and I found ourselves alone for dinner. I decided I'd treat us to carry-out. Actually, I can talk myself into carry-out anyday there's air in the atmosphere. And it's a very short conversation. Something like, "Carry-out?" "Okay."

Brian was absorbed in late afternoon cartoons, so I instructed him to stay put while I drove six blocks to the hot dog place. The trip to the place, as well as the order and pick-up part, went without hitch.

Two blocks from my home, there is a rise in the road. One never knows what awaits on the down side of the rise. Traffic bolts along swiftly during rush hour in this 40 m.p.h. zone and most drivers assume that everything is all clear. I, however, living so close to this accident-waiting-to-happen area, always approach with caution. It's a good thing; ahead in my lane was a stopped commuter bus. A string of cars made it impossible for me to pass, so I was forced to stop a couple car lengths behind. Now I knew where the expression "sitting duck" came from, and what it felt like to be one.

Suddenly, a speeding car flew over the rise and smashed into me. The driver didn't even brake. Thankfully, I had allowed those couple car lengths; otherwise, I would have been sandwiched.

A gentleman who had stepped off the bus a few seconds before the impact witnessed the drama and ran to my aid, as did the guy who hit me. Others gathered around, everyone asking if I was okay.

"My head." That was all I could say. Someone asked if I needed an ambulance. "No, I just need to sit here a minute." I looked in my rear view mirror and saw the car that hit me; it was smoking and in a tangle. I realized then just how great the impact had been. I pinched myself to see if, in fact, I might be dead. I highly recommend you don't pinch yourself when you already have a headache; I was not dead and now everything hurt.

"I have to get home. I only live a couple blocks from here and my son is home alone. I have to get home," I repeated. Visions of Oprah shows and news clips revealing mothers who abandon their kids started ripping through my mind.

"You're in no shape to drive," the guy who'd stepped off the bus said. "Move over, I'll take you home. I live right down the street." Even though this man was a total stranger, the suggestion seemed like the right thing to do. He spoke briefly with the guy who'd hit me, and planned for him to follow us so we could exchange additional information.

As we entered my driveway, the guy driving my car suddenly realized that the other guy had ditched us. He noticed this just in time to see the ditcher turning on to Main Street.

"That blankety-blank-blank!" my driver said. With that, he threw the car in reverse, backed out of my driveway, and floored it. It was then I noticed the smell of alcohol.

Great! My rescuer had been drinking, and we were in a chase.

"Please, just take me home," I moaned, while I cupped both hands around the back of my neck.

"Not 'til we catch that blankety-blank-blank!" he responded, gunning the engine. "We gotta at least get his license plate number," he said.

I was beginning to realize this was a very bad situation indeed. You can't fool me.

Ahead of us, the guy who hit me had just made it through the yellow light at the busy intersection of Main Street and Route 64, an Interstate highway. My driver stepped on the gas.

"No! Take me home," I whimpered. Although my head felt like it was going to explode, my brain was still alert enough to invent news items: "Police involved in high-speed chase through suburbs. It is reported that Charlene Baumbich abandoned her son and husband and ran off with a strange drunken man. Details at six." Lord, help me; hear my prayer. Now.

Finally, my driver snapped to his senses just before blowing through the red light into four lanes of moving traffic. We waited in silence for the light to change, then traveled around the block before he dropped me off. Parking my car, he walked me into my home, asked me if I'd be all right, and disappeared down the street, never to be seen again. Brian looked up from the TV long enough to ask me for his hot dog.

As it turned out, the guy who hit me called several hours

later. He explained that he didn't know where we'd gone, although there didn't seem to be any way that was possible unless he was driving while comatose. It occurred to me that possibly he'd been drinking, too, and had disappeared long enough to sober up. He offered to pay all my expenses, including a trip I assured him I would be taking to the doctor's office the next morning to see about my throbbing head.

He wanted to pay in cash, and he did. I had to wear a neck brace for a couple weeks because I had serious whiplash. And wouldn't you know, this occurred right before a big exposé on television about people who weren't really injured during accidents, but who wore neck braces to collect insurance money. No one believed my outrageous (but true) story; no one believed I was truly injured. I got no respect. But I eventually healed.

I will forever be grateful this accident did not squelch my zest for carry-out food. Sometimes George calls before he leaves work to ask if I need anything, and to inquire what's for dinner, I give him the good news.

"It's your lucky day. Pick up whatever you have a taste for. And since I really love you, Honey, I'll even go get it myself if you're tired. But if traffic is bad, why risk it. We'll simply have it delivered."

16 High Adventure in the Garage

Today I went mountain climbing. Although I have tackled steeper and loftier inclines in my lifetime, I have never encountered one that elicited such emotions.

You see, out of necessity, I climbed the Brown Car. The Brown Car that has been parked—*buried*—in our garage for the last five years. During that time it has metamorphosed into a giant shelf, a shelf like a ship buried at sea and covered with barnacles. Barnacles that turned this once-cherished spiffy new vehicle into a flat-tired, dead-batteried, broken-windshielded, heaped-up sore spot in our marriage.

The reason for my daring climb? To get to the other side. Literally. It was the only way to retrieve the shovel. Good thing George wasn't home. I was blowing fire through my nose by the time I scaled and rappelled the multi-layered hazard.

The Brown Car symbolizes procrastination. Its reputation

has spread throughout the neighborhood and beyond.

When neighbors are asked when they plan to do something they don't want to do they respond: "When George sells the brown car." Ah, the blessed comeback that delivers an even deeper message: probably never.

This once beauty is a 1983 Buick LeSabre. Four doors. Six cylinders. Power door locks but no power seats or windows. Okay radio but no tape deck. Automatic transmission with no kick when you punch in. Basic. Stable. The odometer announces that the Brown Car has seen nearly 100,000 hard-earned miles. It needs new tires and the "Service Engine Soon" light comes on when you start it. Of course, you have to charge the deader-than-dead battery first to see the "Service Engine Soon" light in action.

We bought the Brown Car off the showroom floor, thinking we had "arrived." Wire wheel covers said it all. Yup, we were two wild thaaangs. Five years later, however, George received a company vehicle and my Dad gave Brian his pickup truck. Our other car yielded a more comfortable ride for our mid-life backs and so we parked the Brown Car.

And then its insurance ran out. And then its license plates expired. And then its battery went dead. And then, get this, it ran out of gas! Sitting in the garage! George had charged it, turned it over, and revved it up so many times that it ran out of gas. And then the left rear tire went flat. And then something got thrown on the driver's side of the windshield, cracking it.

All this time, George was "getting ready to sell it." For several months he just couldn't find a "For Sale" sign. Once, a couple years ago, he actually put an ad in the newspaper. Everyone who called laughed after hearing how many miles it had, especially considering George's price.

New tactic: Wash the car before putting it at the end of

the drive baring the sign he finally found. But nay, the battery was dead again and he couldn't back it out to wash it.

Tick, tock, tick, tock. Calendar months and years whizzed by; the Brown Car continued to depreciate. George kept mumbling about the thousands it was *really* worth.

In the meantime, the Brown Car took up one-half of our two-car garage. It stayed nice and dry in the winter while we scraped ice and jockeyed the rest of our vehicles.

One day, someone actually rang our doorbell and asked to buy it! But George said he had to do this and he had to do that and he had to look up this AND that to find out what would be a fair price and... meanwhile, that heaven-sent Angel bought another vehicle. Silently, George sighed with relief. I swear, he even smiled at the news.

I've begun to see a pattern in these past years. I've begun to see that the Brown Car is here to stay. It's probably not worth selling. So instead of whining about its presence, I've rerouted my energy into finding a place to store it. Just like the baby stuff we keep in the attic "just in case." We've had it so long now that we've decided to keep it for our grandchildren. Might as well add the Brown Car to that list of treasures.

Frankly, there'd be a hole in our lives if we no longer had the Brown Car to launch so many lively discussions. Its departure might traumatize those who use it to justify their own procrastinations, including me. The Brown Car, in its own dirt-laden, quiet way, exemplifies the many incomplete projects in my life. Projects that I'm going to get to one day. Projects that have become part of my comfortable chaos. Projects that assure me I have a reason to wake up the next day.

And you know what they say: When you live with someone long enough, you start to become like them. I'm even beginning to ask those "What if?" questions. "What if Brian's truck died?" "What if George had to change jobs?" "What if the other car became disabled?"

Hey! Not to worry! We can always resurrect the Brown Car! It's our security blanket. You know, I believe that's why my husband has found it impossible to let go of that little corner of his world. There's something comforting about just knowing it's there. Just in case.

Just in case we get the urge to indulge in a new experience. Like mountain climbing.

17 The Merry-Go-Round of Life

My friend Larry Turner wrote a poem that gets right to the heart of something that's been consuming the brain power of my dearly beloved George and me. Here's the poem, called "The Bed:"

Each May the bed moves
to catch the breeze
between window and open door.
Each October it moves back
to its protected place
against the far wall.

The years grow shorter.
The bed barely stops at one place
before it returns to the other.
In ever shrinking years
it spins about the room
faster, faster.*

*Note: From Larry Turner's *Stops on the Way to Eden and Beyond* (Naperville, Pugdog Press, 1992). Used by permission.

Ah, yes, the passing of time, the shortening of years, the changes we make, the whirlwind we live in. And thus our scenario. But it isn't the beds that seem to spin in our house, it's our *bedrooms*.

When George and I married, I came ready-equipped with a four-year-old. We purchased a three-bedroom house: one for us, and the other two for Bret and however many more blessings might come along. The first bedroom assignments were dictated via unselfish, practical thinking.

George and I got the middle-size room because it had the biggest closet and a window through which we could ponder while gazing at the backyard. We were newlyweds and pondering was just so romantic!

Bret got the largest room with the medium closet because, if we had bundles of kids, we'd need the biggest room to pack, stack, and stuff them into. We probably wouldn't be able to afford many clothes anyway, so the smaller closet would be just fine.

The small bedroom with its tiny closet would serve as the nursery for our sweet-smelling darlings. But in the meantime it doubled as a left-over-from-moving junk room for fifteen months until Brian was born. We deposited the boxes of stuff in the attic to make way for our shiny new baby. Those boxes remain up there to this day. And we haven't a clue what's in them, but we don't seem to have needed any of it.

As it turned out, Bret and Brian are the sum total of our children. Brian's smiling elephant and hippopotamus wallpaper eventually came down when our occasionally smell-good nursery was transformed into a preteen's smell-bad place to hurl clothes and deposit rocks and half-eaten sandwiches.

What we didn't have was a family room. Or maybe I should say we didn't have a formal living room. Upon entering the front door we were in the only place where we could hang out, aside from the kitchen. Our hangout room housed a television, some great knickknacks, a couple side chairs, and, most importantly, a couple reclining chairs in which, as Brian says, his parents "assume the position" for power lounging; each reclined in our own comfy chair with a popcorn bowl in our laps.

Upon turning the corner by the fireplace wall, you enter the dining room. If you keep turning right, you come to the kitchen. Turn right again and you're back in the hang-out room. (We chase our dog around this circular path, which is how he—and we—get our exercise. Sometimes when he's out of eyeshot he reverses and we wind up meeting head-on. Fun for the feeble minded.) Oh, and of course, the basement, with its life-time cleanup job lurking down there—along with Lord only knows what else. But one room began to own importance, when, in a finger snap, Bret was grown, graduated, and moving out.

For the first few weeks his deserted room served as a shrine that I went into to weep. Then one day, I saw The Room through new eyes: a place for someone (Me, me, oh let it be me!) to sit quietly while everyone else was downstairs. It didn't take me long to box up a few things and move around the furniture to make the room less bedroomy. And I had my place—for about two weeks.

Then Brian saw a new possibility for The Room: HIS! A month of grumbling followed. I held my ground, until a Brady Bunch rerun riddled me with guilt. Even the Brady kids got to move up a notch when one moved out. Brian moved into The Room.

His vacated room became the new sitting room for about

a week until I saw a new possibility: MY OFFICE! I could launch a writing career. And so it became, and so I did.

Now Brian is grown and has moved out. Once again, the rooms just don't seem right. Shouldn't George and I finally have the largest bedroom? Why should I have my ever-increasing office stuff cramped into the smallest room? Wouldn't that old nursery/preteen hangout/office be a cute little sitting room? Sounds like an easy switch, right?

But an underlying saga toughens the decision. As water spreads to fill its available space, so have George and I. (And I'm not talking waist lines, although I could be.)

You see, when Brian departed for college, he left a queen-size water bed. He also left behind a mother with chronic sciatica problems and a father and dog who simultaneously began to snore. After a couple years of being awakened by a snoring husband and snoring dog and finding I was always kicking the wrong one at 2 A.M., one morning I discovered a haven in Brian's warm, cushy, and QUIET water bed. And the next night the same thing occurred to me. And then the next. And then I began my night there.

George didn't wake me up when he came to bed because he went into our room. He also didn't wake me up when, at 5 A.M., he flipped on the overhead light to get ready for work. And George wasn't awakened by my nightly kicking and thrashing. We were, in unspoken comfort, catching on to something the upper class Europeans have known for years: Separate bedrooms are kind of swell! And a couple doesn't have to *sleep* together in the same bed at night to enjoy delightful intimacies. In fact, if one has actually *slept* well at night, one finds intimacies more enjoyable!

As I write this, I'm beginning to see that perhaps a decision has—by default, convenience, and perked-up intimacies—

already been made. Perhaps our rooms have stopped spinning after all. At least for now.

Of course, kids have a way of recycling back home. Perhaps we should always be ready for one more ride on the merry-go-round.

18 Techno Babble

I've had a few occasions arise that hurled me into a quest for cutting edge technology. Then again, one might refer to it as the crimped crease of archaic design, depending on your salesperson and their amenability to your desire to upgrade, yet cling to cognitive understanding.

Having a home office is a catalyst for much of my electronic angst. One of my most recent bouts of Technologically Induced Mental Mania (TIMM) was triggered by telephones. In fact, several rounds of telephone troubles have aimed their ammunition my way. My only consolation is that I'm not alone. Every time I engage in telling someone about my latest fiasco, they have five stories of their own. In fact, I bet you start talking to this book after reading a couple of mine.

You: You think that's something. Wait 'til I tell you about this.

Book: Silence.

You: (Scene 2. Stage right. Dark corner of mental institution—hours later.) You're slumped into a little wad, holding your ears because someone heard you talking to the book and had you carted away. Obsessed, you just kept talking, trying to cleanse yourself of all the irritations, muzak tunes, disconnections, garbled fax messages, and answering machine marathons that still swam in your head. Meanwhile, similar diatribes begin spouting from the people who strapped on your straight jacket, forcing you to listen to them since you can't escape. And they all sound like pre-recorded voice messages that don't respond to human utterings.

Technology. Just typing the word launched me into cyberspace, wherever that is.

A couple months ago I put an office line in. My home phone line just couldn't handle everything I needed it to do: modem, business calls, answering machine, fax, e-mail....

Actually getting the second line wasn't too difficult; a handy friend helped us install it. However, it took several visits to phone stores, and multiple phone calls with other home office people, to try to figure out the actual mechanics of the situation. Which line should the answering machine be on? Did I care if business calls came in on my home line? (I didn't really want to have to change all my letter head and business cards.) Should the fax machine be on standby? How would I recognize its ring? Or did I even want to know if and when it was ringing?

As it turned out, I was forced to leave the fax ringer off because the number for my new business line had been freshly abandoned by someone who let their dog run loose and he was still running, and people were still mad. Each time I'd turn the ringer on, the phone immediately started ringing with angry people calling about all kinds of mad things. You'd think they'd be tired of the fax signal by now.

After much consternation, deliberation, and hair pulling, I decided to get a two-line phone for my office. The answering machine would stay on the home phone in the kitchen because that's where George is used to looking for it. Besides, that combination phone and answering machine and recorder was relatively new, and I hadn't recovered from that last TIMM bout yet. All the digital versus tape, two tapes versus one, separate answering machine versus built-in, and stuff like that could very easily trigger another attack.

Okay, stay with me here: The kitchen phone/answering machine/recorder stayed in the kitchen; the two-line phone went in my office and the phone on the fax stayed dormant.

Then I realized it would also be wise to have the business line in the kitchen because I often get myself a drink or snack or stare out the window into my back yard when I'm on business calls. Nothing personal, just a habit. So the old office phone got hung on the wall in the kitchen right above the old (but relatively new) combo home phone-answering machine that sat on a stand. Thus, the set-up for disaster.

One unsuspecting day, I initiated a call from my kitchen on my business line and was chatting away when, Riiiiing. Riiiiing. "Hold on. It's my other line," I said to Call Number One. I pushed the hold button and set the cradle on my left shoulder.

"Hello" I said to Caller Number Two on my home phone. The person identified herself, but before I could say, "I'll call you back," my call waiting signal rang in.

"Hold on, please," I said to Caller Number Two. I pushed the flash button and said "Hello" to Caller Number Three.

My head was swimming. I couldn't think. I was breaking a sweat, and all I could think to say to Caller Number Three was, "Hold on a moment, please." I set that phone cradle on my right shoulder and tried to pull myself together. I felt like I was living the Who's On First comedy routine.

I ended up taking everyone's number and said I'd call them back, even the first person whom I'd called. It occurred to me that, while I was engaged in decorating myself with cradles and cords, I still didn't have enough lines to operate my fax or my modem at that particular moment. Amazing.

But I truly became amazed when I opened my mailbox and received three phone bills on the same day: home line, business line, and car phone. "The phone company owns me," I said to George. He groaned. The sum total of those bills is as incomprehensible as trying to figure out how it happens that my toilet seat seems to be mysteriously wired to my phone line. The minute my backside hits the circle, the phone rings.

You know, there's something to be said for an outhouse in the country. Away from the hustle and bustle. And the telephone.

19 Club Sweat

Any day now, George and I are going to take a marvelous trip. I'll be walking every step of the way; he will be rowing.

Oh, the places we'll go, and the toning and strengthening we'll achieve, all in our basement while our bodies work out and our minds ride to healthfulness. You see, we are the proud owners of a rowing machine and a treadmill. Oh, and we also have one of those jumpy things that looks like a round, miniature trampoline, so maybe we'll hop a few miles, too. After all, healthy is good. Svelte is in. And exercise is not only popular, it's something we can do together.

But first we must peruse the possibilities. Master the maneuvers. Tame the technicalities. Delve into discipline. Stop the rhetoric and activate the garden slug that lurks in both of us. Trying to begin an exercise program when you're an old married couple can boggle the mind. Jump ropes, electronic bicycles, step aerobics, videos.... The staggering options grow by the advertising minute.

Of course, some options can be eliminated if you have children in college or are on a tight budget. The first is expensive health clubs. Not only are there annual fees, but those bright, multi-layered spandex outfits cost bucks, not to mention the cool gym bags and appropriate shoes. And let's face it, no matter how trendy we try to be, we're... not.

Just the other day my only jeans that fit tore right at the bottom of my buttocks and inner thigh. You might be thinking that I'm in style now. After all, teenagers and young adults are paying extra for jeans with fashionable rips. And the grunge look is in. However, trendy folks do not have cellulite oozing through their rips and settling like a wad of silly putty on the chair next to them.

Several years ago I won a year's membership to a weight-training club. I donned my leotards and went once. My trainer explained what I should achieve on the first of several torture machines. Even with zero weight on that first upper-body apparatus, I couldn't bring my arms together. With defeat and humility, I asked if my strong husband could take over my membership. "Non-transferable." George sighed at the news; I don't believe it was the sound of disappointment. Thankfully, my membership expired.

After a recuperation period, we then decided the cheapest option would be to take Wonderdog Butch on a walk every evening. Experts say a twenty-minute walk done regularly is a good place to begin. But no sidewalks, no good weather, and no cooperation from our disobedient, lunging, and entangling mutt soon dissuaded us from this budding idea, but our gymnastic minds kept flexing for new options.

Shortly thereafter, my grandmother died and left me a small amount of money. "I know, George. I'll get us one of those rowing machines." And so I did. I rowed once and my sciatica screamed at me. Grandma's been gone four years now; that's about how long the rowing machine with the broken roller has sat, untouched, in the corner.

Since we began our quest for fitness, we've heard about lots of "just right" pieces of exercise equipment that now lurk in people's bedroom corners camouflaged by clothing they've flung on the convenient handlebars. Just the other day I clipped a personal ad from the local paper: "Soloflex with attachments $500, Trek 760 with turbo trainer $250," followed by a phone number. Gosh. Attachments, trainers, turbo stuff. Sounds downright painful, doesn't it? I didn't make the call.

But with relentless pursuit, George and I scanned the video counters for just the right exercise program. Many caught his eye. Not because of promised benefits, but because of the "art work" on the boxes. Personally, I cannot understand why anyone would want to actually have buns of steel. Buns of *steel?* Can you imagine plopping down at your desk and hearing a sound reminiscent of The Gong Show? You'd probably shatter your teeth.

And so we purchased two Richard Simmons' exercise videos. I used them sweating to the oldies on more than one occasion. But after actually viewing the tapes, Big George decided he just wasn't ready to clap those hands and jive; he decided to fix the rowing machine instead.

Meanwhile my stress level (partly induced by the guilt caused by all the exercise we weren't getting) was calibrating at the high end of the scale. Since exercise is a known stress defuser, it was time to stop dawdling and just do it. Walking still seemed the least taxing on the body; treadmill talk began; shopping followed; the treadmill arrived. George said I should figure it out and then tell him how to use it. Seemed like a good idea to me.

Lesson number one: Never use new exercise equipment when you're home alone, especially if it's electronic. By the time I finished reading the directions, I was exhausted. Straddle the belt. Attach heart monitor to ear. Determine miles-per-hour and all other settings. Attach safety shut-off to clothing. (I should have paid more attention to this last one.)

I hurled myself off the conveyor belt on more than one occasion. After I told George about my adventures, he wanted to install a floor-height phone next to the treadmill so we could dial 911 from the splat position. Like the little trooper my dad raised me to be, however, I climbed back on that bronco and now have tamed it, although I don't ride often enough.

George and I are once again in the "we're-not-kidding" planning stages of exercising together. And we're *not kidding*. We're already burning calories by flapping our jaws talking about the great and wondrous journeys we plan to take. He will row; I will walk. Perhaps a few tunes in the background will enhance our healthy togetherness and create an enchanted atmosphere for our thrice-weekly departure.

Others can talk about their need to stop by the club or their latest aerobic class. But as for me and my honey, we're gonna travel. By hook or by crook, we're gonna conquer this exercise thing together. And although we may not end up with buns of steel, we have high hopes that our rewards will at least produce bellies of laughter and years of health.

20 Two Cannibals in Love

Every Halloween I take time to reminisce about George and my first Halloween as a couple.

With the "I do's" less than two weeks behind us, the invitation arrived. It created quite the excitement for us two love-doves for a couple of reasons: It was the first mail Mr. and Mrs. George Baumbich received; isn't EVERYTHING just WONDERFUL when you are first married?

We decided to go as cannibals. Yes! We would be Mr. and Mrs. Cannibal. We would take the energy from our wildly soaring love, channel it into unbridled creativity, and be assured of no less than the grand prize at the "Absolutely No One Admitted Without A Costume!" party.

Task number one: Gather a million bones. We would tie them in our hair, hang them around our waists, and arm ourselves with the club-like ones. Although the butchers probably thought we were destitute, we were the happy campers after a fruitful hunt.

Task number two: Boil the meat off dem bones. We stood over the boiling cauldron together, holding hands all the while.

Task number three: Decide what we would wear with the bones. We meandered around a fabric shop until happening on the perfect jungle material. It was my moment to dazzle my caveman with my deftness at the sewing machine.

With astonishing flair, I wrapped the material around us and started pinning, like I knew what I was doing. Snip, sew a straight line, snip again. *Voila!* Cannibal costumes. (Who really knows what one's supposed to look like anyway? The only thing I knew for sure, thank goodness, is that they weren't supposed to look tailored.)

Next, we dropped some big bucks at a gag shop: shrunken heads for me to wear as earrings, plastic fangs for our grins, black grease paint, and a bag of feathers. Feathers adorned the poison dart blowers we crafted out of cardboard tubes that come on hangers from the cleaners. Clever, eh? (Giggles.)

And what would a cannibal be without a spear? Ominous-looking arrows were tooled out of tin foil, then firmly anchored to ruthless broom sticks. Wicked! (Hugs and kisses.)

More miscellaneous doo-dads were tied, stuck, and pinned about us in a flurry of final touches. I grabbed a couple of my "falls" (fake hair pieces that were big in the 60s), and we laced them with the bones for scalps. Grease paint war stripes, mixed with menacing hues of sparkling eye shadow, set the final stage for our arm-in-arm gander in the mirror.

We were, without exaggeration, sensational. We were, in no underestimation, authentic. We were, undoubtedly, winners. (Very strange fanged kisses.)

And so we made our way to the car. We strolled ever so slowly to the parking lot from our second-floor apartment, hoping we would run into every tenant in the building for some oohs, aahs, and cheering.

Although the party was only two towns away, the drive seemed to take hours because we were so anxious to make our grand entry. We entertained ourselves and the rest of the traffic by making our scary personas obvious while stopped at red lights.

At last we arrived. We paused outside the door for last-minute adjusting, then readied our weapons.

"Ding-dong, ding-dong, ding-dong."

As soon as the door was opened wide enough, we leaped in screaming, "Kowabunga!"

"Surprise! Surprise!" echoed back at us. Laughter filled the room.

We slowly lowered our spears and dart blowers. Our eyes tried to drink in what surrounded us: a room full of friends, not one wearing a costume, and all wearing dresses, suits, and ties.

"What's going on?" George quietly asked the host, who was right next to us, doubled over with laughter.

"It's a surprise wedding shower for you guys!" his wife finally eeked out.

So there we stood. The best doggone cannibals in the country. We had definitely been tricked—and treated.

21 It May Be Chaos, but It's Mine

Every woman likes to have Her Space. I, however, seem to need My Space Here and My Space There. I even seem to need My Space in Your Space on hormone-rushing days.

One of the spaces I occupy most often is my ten-by-ten office. It's disorganized, dusty, it's dripping with signs and photos and papers papers papers. It houses my ink well collection, a piece of bark with words made out of macaroni, a piece of art that Bret made in day camp eons ago. Beside it, a plaque that says "Never try to teach a pig to sing. It wastes your time and annoys the pig." It has necessities such as a clock and a thingie that when you blow into it, makes that obnoxious raspberry sound. I blow it often because that's how I'm feeling. Other musical instruments include a harmonica I want to learn to play and the mouthpiece to a saxophone I'd like to buy one day. And learn how to play. And candles, of course, and on and on and I love it.

I love this space, except on days when I'm tripping over all my stuff, and then I think I need to move My Space to a bigger space. I tell George, "I just need more space to organize my stuff," but we both know that would never really happen.

I have actually cleaned my office space a few times. I mean *really* cleaned it. As opposed to the times when I just stack things up and give it a quick swipe. But more typically, my office is where I throw everything when company comes because I can close the door. There's no reason for anyone to see my office (unless they're snooping around upstairs when they use the bathroom, in which case they *deserve* to see the mess).

Of course, they probably wouldn't be upstairs in the bathroom because we have a downstairs bath. No matter how I time it, I'm always running late, and it's always the upstairs bathroom I don't get to before company arrives. So, when someone heads that way, I yell, as their foot is mid-way up step two, "No! Use the one down here!"

This is when I unknowingly infringe upon George's space; the space in his brain where he logs items that store up before exploding. One day when we were grumbling about something unrelated to cleaning, George delivered a punch below the belt. He hollered, I mean he *hollered*, "And after 25 years, what do you think people think is *in* that upstairs bathroom!" I have no answer to that, but obviously, I know something George doesn't know: Every household has its room(s) that don't get entered when company comes. Right?

Recently, however, we had a doubly-whammy experience: four three-day, overnight guests. Every available space (and especially My Space and My Hidden Space) would need to be utilized. One of the single young men would have to sleep in my office on a chair that unfolds into a bed; obviously six people would need both bathrooms.

The Good Book says all our days are numbered. Getting my office ready for someone to sleep in it (a tall someone who could see the top shelves when standing and the low ones when sleeping) removed three days from the space of my life.

That was three weeks ago. You should see my space now.

I mean, "Don't go up there! It annoys the pig."

22 Long Distance Love

One week from tomorrow, I will be leaving on a week's vacation, alone. Although this will not be the first time my husband and I have been apart, it will go down as the first time in our marriage that we have not been together on my birthday or our anniversary.

I decided to spend my birthday in a state where I've never been.

Oh, not that George doesn't get me wonderful cards, buy hinted-for presents, and treat me to dinner out, but last year, the first year with an empty nest, I found myself wandering about the house, becoming melancholy about birthdays past.

This behavior, I decided, was not going to be repeated.

In my haste and excitement (and perhaps a bit of selfishness), I had forgotten (or had I?) that our anniversary would also be swallowed by mydeparture. When I first realized this, after the "no refunds or changes" reservations were made, my heart started racing. What would George think? What had I done?

That night at dinner I told him about my plans to finally get out to the West coast. He was pleased. Seeing my excitement, he acknowledged my enthusiasm. I told him when I would be gone and what that would encompass. He paused for a moment, fork mid-air, eyes directly on me. Then he responded with an answer that washed me anew with love for him.

"I'm sorry you won't be here for our anniversary, but I'm happier you're getting away. You really need the vacation."

The whole incident has given me pause to consider the importance of our celebrations.

If we don't ceremoniously take time to consider what's behind us—what we have survived, overcome, laughed about, cherished, and sometimes simply plowed through with gritted teeth—if we don't take time to reflect on this progress and celebrate its very existence, what's the point?

I'm not talking grand ballroom and violins (although if you're reading this, George, I'm open to that), but rather a set-aside time to look each other in the face and say, "Hey, we're making it. Another year has passed and we still love each other."

Let us observe and record the marking of these times. Put another notch on the front of our wedding album. Bow our heads. Lift our voices. Give each other a big smooch right on the lips, right in front of the kids and our flea-bag dog and everybody!

Sure, we've all had those Christmases and anniversaries and birthdays that have run amuck: expectations too high, burnt dinners, rude guests, illness, and incredibly tasteless gifts.

But even those occasions give us something to laugh about and remember as we saunter through life. They become a part of what we bring forward with us, into the next celebration.

Last year we hadn't made plans for our anniversary. All our resources (emotional and monetary) had gone into sending our baby off to college just two weeks previous.

Then friends called and said, "How about a Cub game on the 20th. We've got free tickets."

"Great! That's our anniversary!" we said.

They doubled our enthusiasm by offering to share the gift certificate they had received from a trendy, casual restaurant downtown.

We had a super time. I even coaxed George into one of those put-a-dollar-in photo booths. Sitting on his lap, we both laughed, made dumb faces, and scrambled between flashes to look even more dumb or dreamy. We now have a one-inch photo of us kissing. I bought little tiny frames and keep these funny treasures on my dresser to remind us that we can still act crazy.

An anniversary celebration of different characteristics took place three years after we were married. We had just spent days cleaning out a flooded basement; we were depressed and tired.

Parents to the rescue! They sent us a three-day, two-night package at a poshy hotel. What a blessing! We ate French food while a harpist serenaded in the background. George and I lifted our glasses and toasted our new-found perspective: We were okay. That's what really mattered. It was one of our most luxurious and momentous celebrations.

And that is partially why I can leave on my vacation to Oregon this year. George and I have celebrated a lot throughout our marriage, marking time in style, and with passionate remembrance. We have harvested and partaken of the celebratory fruits of our labor, and the bounty shall keep us comfortably full until I return.

23 Steaming in the Southwest

Vacations are wonderful for an old married couple. Two people, sharing an adventure, seeing the sights, being together nearly every minute, becoming acutely aware they don't like the same activities, working on different time clocks, being trapped in the car together for hours on end.... Whoops!

Okay, so after many years some of the vacation glow may be gone, but that doesn't mean you can't fan the embers and look for suitable compromises. Right?

So with bellows pumping, George and I headed off alone together from Albuquerque (where we were visiting family) to Santa Fe (where yet more tourists were) for a two-day romantic respite. Maybe we'd even take a drive up to Taos.

We didn't get out of Albuquerque until late afternoon and I was hungry; we'd eaten a late breakfast and just never got around to lunch. Hunger brings out the extra bad of my worst side(s). Trust me on this. George wanted to check into our motel before eating. Usually he's good about stopping when I need to, but this day found him a man with a mission. Before we got to the Super 8, I was whining.

"George, do you know that no matter where we go in this country, it looks the same because we always stay at a Super 8? I know they have clean, dependable rooms and are in our budget, but what's the point of traveling half way across the country to see the same thing every place we go? Milwaukee, Minnesota, San Francisco, and now Santa Fe will all feel the same when I go to bed. Why, George, can't we stay in a different place just once in a while? A place that... blah blah blah."

George finally spoke. "What road is the Super 8 on? Are you looking at the map? Is this where we exit?"

"George, you're not listening to a word I say."

"Yes I am. You're complaining about why we always stay in a Super 8."

"Right. So?"

"So remember the time the Super 8 was full in Winona? That other place costs us $98. And for what? A bed?"

"No, George. It had a whirlpool bathtub and a swimming pool. It had a sauna and a weight room. It had a game room and cable. It had continental breakfast. It felt like vacation."

"I'd rather spend the money on something else. What do we do in the room anyway? Get in late, go to sleep, and then get up early and go eat because you're hungry, right? We're barely in the room. Why pay big bucks for a bed?"

"George, maybe we'd spend more time in the room if it were a little nicer. More exciting. More exotic. Get my drift?"

"Is this where we turn? I'm turning."

"George, you just don't care what I think, do you?"

"Yes, I care."

"But we're staying at the Super 8 anyway, right?"

"Right."

The ride to the Super 8 was quiet. I'm sure George was happy. We found it without much trouble, took our bags to the room, went to the desk, and asked about the location of a very close place to eat, The desk clerk recommended a "nice family restaurant right down the street." Back into the car we went, down the four-lane divided highway toward the middle of town. Before we'd ventured very far, I spotted it.

"There it is, George. Get in the other lane."

"I see it."

"George! Get in the other lane."

"I'll handle it. I can't pull over right now. There's a car coming up."

"You can't pull over right now because there's a car coming up because you didn't pull over back there when I first told you to. Now you're going to miss the turn." I said as we whizzed by the restaurant.

Two things are at work here: one, I was starving, not hungry, but starving; and two, George is always in the wrong lane. It's a miracle he found the right shoot at birth.

After traveling several blocks before we could turn around and finally get back to the restaurant, I had done a lot of internal talking. *Shut up, Charlene. You're on vacation. Just because George drives like a Gomer doesn't mean you have to keep chiding. What's the point of arguing? Does it get you anywhere faster?*

And so we entered the restaurant on a quiet, but hungry, note. We were the only ones there. If there was an atmosphere more hostile than our little family, it was this little family restaurant. It permeated the place.

Finally we asked if they were open.

"Yes!" snapped a woman. She headed for the seating area without offering so much as a "follow me." We sat across from one another trying to ignore the fact that an older woman was cleaning tables and seat covers and flinging the chairs around. Seriously. They were nearly airborne.

In the meantime, the woman who had seated us was on the phone. Screaming. "You don't appreciate a thing I do for you! You can't even pick up when I ask you too. I can't believe…!"

George and I decided our own friction was enough for us. It was emotionally too hot in there. We left.

Now we had no plan for a restaurant. George spotted a nearby McDonalds and suggested we eat there.

"First we have to stay at a Super 8, then you want me to travel half way across the country to eat at McDonalds?"

"I thought you were starving."

"I am, but for vacation food."

"Where do you want to eat?"

"I don't know. Just head toward the square. How many miles are we from the square anyway? Super 8s are always on the outskirts of town. Wouldn't it be nice if we could occasionally just walk to a restaurant? Maybe even eat in our hotel lobby?"

"Well you can't. Just tell me where you want to go." As soon as those words left George's mouth, a thought occurred to him. "Hey, didn't we get a sheet of coupons from the rental car place? Didn't they say, 'If you get to Santa Fe, here's some coupons for free hors d'oeuvres?'"

"Yes," I said, in my starving, weakened state. I began thrashing through the glove compartment. "Here it is." I read him a list of about eight restaurants. "What do you have a taste for?"

"I don't care. What do you want? You're the one who's hungry."

"Italian. Pasta sounds real good," I chirped.

"I don't have a taste for Italian."

"Then don't tell me to pick a place! Where do you want to go?"

"I'm driving. I can't read the map. Just pick something and tell me what lane to get into."

Finally I decided on Thai food. I looked location number six up on the coupon map and tried to get a read on the next intersection. Of course we were in the wrong lane. Of course we missed our turn—twice. Of course it took us a very long time to finally see the sign. The volume on our voices had escalated to Mach 9.

Finally we pulled up across the street from the place and George began to enter the parking lot. I clutched the door handle for a quick exit.

"Pay parking? I'm not paying to park to go eat!"

"George! You're getting a free appetizer. You're on vacation. Park."

There was no way George was pulling into the pay lot. We cruised around until we found a parking spot with a meter. Gimme a break! Like meters are free?

George went to the meter and plunked in a dime. The red arm in the meter barely made a clinking noise, then registered only twenty minutes. George was furious. Good, we were even.

He put in two more dimes, then asked me how long would it take to eat. Wrong question, George. "If you think I'm cramming down my food now after waiting all this time so you don't have to...." He emptied his pockets of change, stuffed each coin in the meter, and we headed for the restaurant—only to find out they didn't open for another hour.

We slammed our car doors and began another quick study of the map. We settled on the Blue Corn Cafe. It didn't look too far away. One-way, wrong-way, around the block we went.

"There, George. There's a lot."

"What? I'm not paying to park in a lot. I'll find a place. Just be quiet."

The only way I could follow that instructive was to leave the car. I announced I was heading for the restaurant to order a beverage and our free appetizer.

"Fine."

"Fine." I leaped out of the car in the middle of the intersection. Slambang. George peeled off.

I accidentally set off in the right direction. I almost missed it, however, because the entrance was on the corner, and the sign wasn't visible as you looked down the street. The restaurant was upstairs and quite cute. I was seated immediately and was very happy to see a bowl of chips and salsa as soon as my backside hit the chair. I began cramming them into my mouth and could barely speak when the waiter came to take my order. I explained I was waiting for someone, but that we'd like our free appetizer. Two bowls of chips, half the free guacamole, and twenty minutes later, George still had not arrived.

It occurred to me he wasn't able to: 1) remember the name of the restaurant; 2) couldn't find it because of its hidden location; or 3) had headed for Chicago without me.

I called over the waiter and said, "I'm beginning to envision a very bad evening. I'm not skipping out, but I need to leave for a few minutes to find my husband. I'll be back."

Down the stairs I headed, then up and down the street. No George. I decided to stay put; that's what we always used to tell the kids when they were lost.

Suddenly I heard his yelling voice. "Where am I supposed to park?" George's head hung out the window as he passed through the intersection in our two-door, Thunderbird rental car, smoke rolling out his ears, looking every bit the maniacal man. "No one will give me change for the meter and I put it all in the last place!"

I couldn't believe it. He was still driving around trying to avoid the lot. I simply pointed, shook my head, and headed back to the guacamole.

Yes, vacations are a wonderful thing for an old married couple. Two people, sharing an adventure, seeing the sights, being together nearly every minute, becoming acutely aware they don't like the same activities, working on different time clocks, being trapped in the same car together for hours on end....

24 What's Plastic Got to Do With It?

7:00 A.M. I can't believe I had anything to do with selecting the fake Christmas tree swallowing up my living room, but it's true; in fact, I was the instigator. Battle scars from previous years had worn me down. Wars that went like this:

"George, I don't care if this fresh green tree costs $40, we only buy one a year."

"I'm not spending forty bucks on a Christmas tree. It won't fit in the living room anyway. What are you gonna do? Cut three feet off the bottom? Why spend forty bucks buying one this big, and then cut it off? No."

"Mom, here's a nice one," Brian says, dragging his giant of a selection toward the pouting me.

"Brian, that won't fit in the living room."

"Fine. I'll keep looking."

George appears with a shrub. Honestly, it's so small it should have been a house plant, and I tell him so. He tosses it aside and disappears around the corner.

Bret falls in love with a couple trees no one likes,

although my and his tastes seem to be the closest.

And the war continues, turning our tree-buying adventure into an annual family pain in the poinsettia.

We travel to another lot, where all the trees are $12.95. Finally, all worn down, we get "whatever." The tree ends up being so dry that we're afraid to turn the lights on. Every year I threatened to buy a fake one; every year I hated myself for the suggestion.

But this year, everything changed.

As I sit here in the early morning hours staring at the still-naked tree, sipping my second cup of tea, I wonder what's happened to me. How did I stoop to this: an artificial, man-made piece of seasonal greenery that replaces years of sap-running, fragrant tradition? Even if we do get to avoid the tree-lot blues.

Perhaps the slide began last year when, because of a heavy work load, I ran out of time to bake Christmas cookies. Oh, I managed to crank out one batch of cutter-cookies, but not the usual dozens that once consumed all my Tupperware bowls.

Or maybe it snuck up on me the Christmas before last when my oldest son didn't make it home for the holidays. What was the point of creating my usual plethora of stunning bows only to have to smoosh them into flat wads when I packed them? In fact, there was only time for a few curlicues, since I had to make an extra UPS run to send Bret's packages away, instead of hiding them for Santa's appearance.

So here we are, me and this so-called tree. Setting my teacup on the arm of the couch, I uncurl my legs from under me and deliberately move across the room to reshape a few of the stiff wire branches. Task completed, I kneel at the foot of the 7-1/2 foot imitation thing and scan its depths.

The tree becomes a blur as I mourn for Christmases past: dawn-breaking giggles, carrots left by the fireplace for reindeer, endless hours spent in Santa's line slicking hair into place for photos, cookies decorated with fingerprints, broken ornaments... excitement. Even the days of tree wars.

"So," I say to sleeping Butch, sniffing on my way to the kitchen, "it's a three-cup morning." His eyes roll open and focus on me for a moment. "And I deserve one."

My saturated tea bag looks okay. But the fact is, it can make only weak tea now, tea that just isn't satisfying like the first serving. Tea that fills the cup, but somehow isn't really tea.

I pour the brew down the sink after one sip, seat myself in the chair across from the tree, and invite the dog to climb up into my lap.

The sun has come around a bit, brightening the room, breathing a whisper of life into the meticulously-placed branches. I notice for the first time there isn't one needle stuck in the carpet. I won't have to vacuum, I think.

4:00 P.M., with an armful of groceries, I arrive home just as rosy twilight shadows cast their way into my living room, landing on The Tree. We have never brought home such a perfectly-shaped tree. Each limb is balanced and looks sturdy enough to showcase the heavy, gold spray-painted, macaroni ornament our son, Brian, had presented to us so many trees ago.

Yes, when we drag our eight boxes of decorations down from the attic tonight, this humongous tree won't have a lick of trouble harboring our years' worth of homemade treasures.

And I won't have to worry about fires.

It's a good year for an open house, I decide. Within five minutes, I pick the date and make a list of hors d'oeuvres. I'll send invitations with our Christmas cards. I'll bake at least two batches of cookies. After all, I'll have time because I won't be vacuuming needles every day. I'll make a bowl of yuletide punch. This will be the year for a new tradition: fresh garland draped around the place. Fragrant. Inviting. Homey.

"I'll get my picture taken with Santa Claus," I chirp to Butch. He groans, as if disapproving. I scratch his head and fantasize about grandchildren.

My husband and son arrive home and grumble about the tree. We talk about Christmas trees past, including many a Charlie Brown tree, hours of arguing over too fat or tall or small or wide or expensive. We laugh a lot.

We pop frozen pizzas into the oven while unraveling our day's happenings; I unfold my new tradition idea. We quickly unpack the boxes labeled "tree decorations" and consider buying an extra string of lights. The garland idea is a hit, and so is the party.

By evening's end, the tree is spectacular, woven and crammed with pieces of our lives. The halls are decked and sugarplums are doing their warm-ups. It's time to unpack the last box.

Wise men and camels are gently anchored in billows of "angel hair." The Child emerges from the tissue that swaddled him. He gazes at me from the manger.

All is well.

25 Why Coupons Are Ruining My Life

I have this cabinet above my stove that I cannot see into without jumping up in the air. I can reach the bottles stored in front if I stand on my tippy toes, but I cannot see what's behind them. Hence, that cabinet is used to store things I don't use very often. Things such as Tabasco sauce, Worcestershire sauce, steak sauce, soy sauce, red hot sauce, vinegar (apple and white), olive oil, pure sesame oil, cooking sherry, Elmer's glue—and coupons.

Consider this: Relationships (even some blood relationships) have been strained because of those lousy coupons. For instance, I can hardly stand to visit my favorite cousin any more, her and her shoe boxes and file folders neatly organizing volumes of alphabetized coupons. I tell you, her dedication to those cut out, rip off, get-'em-in-the-mail little pieces of paper riddles me with guilt.

And so, no more can I just sit back and relax. I feel obligated to tackle every magazine and evening newspaper with not only my glasses, but a pair of scissors for those nasty "fifteen cents off" bulletins that rear their ugly heads every other paragraph.

George and my diets have been seriously deregulated by boxes and bags of things I would never have plucked off the grocers shelves without the incentive of those devilish enticers.

Should my family ever want to eat out, heaven forbid we should pick a place for which we don't have a coupon. Even if our taste buds are hankering for a nice steak dinner we have often had to swallow down pizza or chicken in response to "large for a medium price" or a "value bucket coupon."

A simple trip to the grocery store can end up in a guilt-ridden sleepless night because I have: 1) left the coupons on the kitchen table; 2) forgotten to hand them to the check-out person; 3) had the checker discover most of them had expired in 1972; or 4) shopped myself into exhaustion at a number of stores because I was determined to have items 1, 2, or 3 but could not find the product.

Our budget, which should be enhanced by coupons, has been dented by coupon accessories. I have purchased three coupon organizers because I always think each will inspire me to organize, which it does not. I also am the proud owner of four nifty coupon clippers that I can't ever find, which is why I own four of them.

Coupons are ruining my life. And if their clutter and guilt-producing powers alone aren't threatening enough, now they've almost killed me—literally. You see, the coupons (and they probably number in the hundreds by now) are up in this cabinet so I don't have to look at them and be exposed to their power. I add to them religiously. I use them, if I am to be honest, almost never.

On a recent dark and stormy afternoon when I was alone in the house and preparing a shopping list, I heard an eery voice say, "You're not seriously going to buy instant coffee without taking one of our more than twenty coupons for instant coffee, are you?" And so, I approached "the cabinet."

Stretching my body to its maximum height, I pushed aside the Worcestershire sauce with my fingertips. A few coupons fluttered to my feet. They were not the coffee coupons; but they were coupons that reminded me that I wanted to try "Golden Goopers with a Tad More Raisins" and "Ebony Toothpaste with Green Fluoride Flecks." I put them next to my shopping list.

A corner of what appeared to be a coffee coupon peeked at me from the far edge of the cabinet. I jumped in the air and grabbed it. Well, the other end of the coupon, unknown to me, was tucked under the can of Crisco and out it tumbled. Practically before my feet hit the floor, the Crisco hit my head. I fell to the floor in agony.

More unfortunate, the Crisco was the main gate behind which hundreds of coupons were tossed. I was soon buried in an avalanche of from "5 cents" to "a dollar off." But this wasn't what almost killed me.

I barely escaped with my life when the very clever "razor blade coupon clipper" sliced its way into the linoleum, an eighth of an inch from my wrist.

I'd like to say this was the end of coupons in my life, that I scooped them up, tossed them in the waste basket (clever organizers and all), and declared a life-long moratorium on them.

But the truth is, coupon mania wins again. The clipper was not only right at my fingertips, but had landed next to the best two-for-one in the bunch.

26 A River Runs Down It

For Christmas last year, Bret gave me a wonderful and very useful gift: a fanny pack (to balance my built-in fanny pack) that holds a drink bottle. Since I am undoubtedly Queen of the Perpetual Drink Sippers, that was, indeed, a handy item.

Before George and I left on our annual trek to the local county fair, I filled 'er up and strapped 'er on. After walking around for about an hour and finishing my second tank full, so to speak, it was time to hit the john. Right now!

Since it was a very hot, sticky day, and since a strapped-on fanny pack makes loosening clothing so much more difficult, I unsnapped it from around my waist and hung it around my neck so I could negotiate the necessities without impairment.

In the nick of time, I was free to do my duty. Whew! But by mid-stream, a horrible sensation struck me. Rather it started running down the inside of my left leg after passing through the crotch of my downed shorts. In the heat and desperateness of disencumbering myself from the tacky clothes, I must not have gotten something pulled down right. To make it worse, it was beyond my capabilities to shut off the tap, so to speak. I was stunned, humiliated, and wet.

Then the light dawned. I hadn't secured the pop-up top on the drink bottle and, since I was bent over and it dangled from my neck, the water poured right into my pants. Although my shorts were a mess, I was relieved to find out that the situation wasn't what I first believed it to be.

But relief was brief because suddenly I saw them—the dancing feet of the lady in the stall next to me. The stream of water that had run down my leg had quickly flowed in her direction. Of course she didn't know the stream had originated from my water bottle, so I quickly hollered, "It's not what you think! It's my water bottle."

My reassurance did nothing to stop those dancing feet that were trying to hover, one at a dancing time, above the floor and out of the stream.

I exited the stall before her and dutifully waited to show her exactly what had happened. I had become nearly hysterical with laughter by this point.

When the lady exited her stall, through peals of laughter, I tried to give her a quick demo as to what had happened. She didn't laugh, she didn't smile, she didn't wash her hands. She simply left me standing alone wearing wet pants, babbling, and laughing.

The next lady who entered the bathroom took a swift up-and-down look at me and didn't laugh either.

Dear Lord, thanks for helping me to laugh at myself. Especially when I'm the only one who thinks I'm funny. Okay, so the joke's on me, but at least I get it!

27 All Cards and Gifts are Welcome

I love birthdays. Yours, mine... even a stranger's in a restaurant. But most of all, I love my birthday. I have no shame about it.

I start reminding people about my birthday the minute we buy the new year's calendar. We're talking a lot of reminding here, because my birthday isn't until September 23rd, usually on the first day of Fall. I'm fond of saying, "I was born and the leaves began to die."

Although all my birthdays are one-of-a-kind, a few pop into my mind. One of them was my twelfth.

We lived on a small farm in Wheaton, Illinois, and I decided to have about a half-dozen girlfriends over to sleep in the barn. We hauled blankets, sleeping bags, chips (I dearly loved chips even at an early age), pop, flashlights, curlers, training bras, and giggles to the top of the hay bales. It was very dark. Very chilly. And we started telling VERY scary stories long before midnight. You know, the kind that involve hooks and axe murderers and haunting sounds and incredibly twisted mind games and....

The scarier and gorier the stories got, the quieter we became. The quieter we became, the louder unknown barn/bat/vampire/ghost/murderer noises grew.

The first to show their fear were scoffed at, but pretty soon their racing hearts could be heard throbbing in the stillness. Before long, even I, the "Bravest of the Brave," was trying very hard to hide the fact that I was becoming slightly paranoid. I envisioned the escaped convict lurking just outside the double barn doors and OHMYGOSH wasn't that something I saw move through the crack and OHMYGOSH why are the pigeons suddenly flying around like they're berserk and....

Within a half-hour, several girls had to go to the bathroom, or so they said. As their baby-doll-pajamaed legs started to leave the barn, the rest of the party found reason to follow. They needed to retrieve another pop, or perhaps one last bag of chips, or maybe they forgot to apply their Noxema. Whatever their excuses, the small pack of wide-eyed girls (the entire party's worth) moved as one unit to the safety of the living room, where we stayed all night without blankets and snacks. And no more stories. Certainly no more stories.

One of the wildest birthday parties I ever had was the one I threw for myself when I turned thirty-nine because it was the last time I wouldn't be forty. And that's exactly what my invitations said. However, who would have ever guessed how the day of my fortieth would begin. When I opened the door in the early morning to retrieve the paper while wearing my nightgown, imagine my surprise when I saw rolls of toilet paper strung from every possible limb God so handily supplied. Our sidewalk leading to the front door announced "Happy 40th Char" in shaving cream. A few rolls of toilet paper were still intact at the top of our Blue Spruce. Creative birds could have simply nested in the middle of the cardboard.

The idea that someone would go to all this trouble and childlike fun just for my birthday, a milestone at which people say nasty things about memory loss, was exquisite. I hoped our street was very busy with traffic and that passersby caught the joyful spirit.

While George and I were guessing who might have gone to all this trouble, we invited our fifty-something friend Marlene over to see this fabulous display and to share a cup of birthday tea. Marlene is one of our best friends. She was stunned. Speculations as to just who this genius was flew left and right.

And then Marlene looked at Wonderdog Butch and, with a playful grin, said, "Some watch dog you are." The secret was out; she had arrived at 4 A.M. to create this Birthday Wonderland, risking tripping in the dark and hurting herself, not to mention arrest! Yes, my fortieth will always be remembered.

Then there was the year Marlene phoned me and said, "Guess who's going to be in Chicago on your birthday? Elizabeth Taylor! She's going to be at Marshall Field's doing a promotion for her new cologne. Let's go."

Since I was a child, I've been told I look like Elizabeth Taylor. Although I've never been able to detect it, it has caused me countless hours of searching in front of the mirror for that certain something that smacks of Liz and makes people approach me, mouths agape, to tell me how they "had to look twice!"

All I can figure is that it's my mole. Rather my beauty mark, as my mother used to call it. And although I don't have violet eyes, my eyes are undoubtedly my best feature, because it certainly isn't my legs or anything else. The idea of staring at Liz to see if she looked like me was intriguing, and so I enthusiastically said okay.

We took the train downtown very early to be among the first in line so we could get an up-close and personal glimpse of her beauty. We actually stood staring at an empty stage for two-and-a-half hours, watching everyone else who thought they looked like Liz preen for her arrival. Also, it occurred to me that beauty demands beauty; who among us wanted to look frumpy?

I'll spare you the details and cut to the punch: I did finally get a glimpse of what others have noticed about the resemblance. It wasn't the straight forward view I'd been searching for in the mirror all these years, but our profile and serious facial expression. Yes, and although my eyes are not violet, they do look like hers, as does my over-all profile and coloring. At least that's where I saw it.

Last year's b-day was one of my more peculiar. I decided I should take an all-day time management seminar being offered on my birthday! Just like the Liz thing. How profound. What a great way to set a new, organized course for myself on the very day of my birth. I could restructure my own personal infrastructure and spend the very day of my birth thinking about what I am doing with my life.

The seminar was held at a large, posh hotel with all kinds of banquet facilities, clubs, and other amenities. I was one of sixty or so attendees. As the day progressed, I learned most of them had been sent by their companies, who recommended (as in you *will* use this) the system, and they even had some custom sections built into their planners.

I introduced myself as The Birthday Girl when the

opportunity arose to answer a question as to why we were there. Nobody sang.

By lunch time, I had to go to the bathroom, real bad. When I was done emptying out so I could fill up, everyone had already left our meeting room. Somehow I had envisioned a couple of interesting people still talking to the teacher; I would meet up with them and find that they were eager to eat lunch with The Birthday Girl.

WRONG! Not only had they dispersed, I didn't have a clue as to what most of them looked like. I hung around the seating area of one of the restaurants hoping someone would notice me and say, "Hey, Birthday Girl, how about sitting together?" Wrong.

And so I ate alone, at a table next to the silverware station. I noticed my table was the only one without a flower, so I requested one—since it was my birthday and I told them so. No one delivered a free dessert, crowded around and sang, or even served me whipped cream. What is this world coming to?

At any rate, I had a chance to think a lot about what I do with my time, compared to what I'd like to be doing with my time, in respects to work and leisure. (I learned I dink around a lot. Bad for work, good for leisure.) All was not lost, and it does a body good to simply stop and remember that our time on earth is limited: what are we doing with it? Hopefully my new *awareness* of what I do with my time will enhance the days to come. Better choices might lead to better memories. Maybe. Then again, I like dinking around.

I couldn't wait to get home so The Birthday Celebration could begin and I could share my new discoveries. What I arrived to was a sleeping dog and a message on the recorder from George that he'd gone to his mother's because he didn't know when I'd be home. Also, no cards in the mail.

I did have wonderful phone conversations with my sons, and I enjoyed telling George about my day later that evening. But that birthday won't go down as one of my favorites.

This year, I don't know what we'll be up to; we've talked about a mini-road trip. But wherever and whatever we're doing, you can be assured those around me will know I'm The Birthday Girl, whether they give a squat or not.

It's not that I enjoy getting a year older, understand. Wider. Wrinklier. Grayer. Slower. I've even heard a lot of people say, "Birthdays? Forget it. Just another day to me. Who needs them?"

I do. The celebration of the gift of life is something I hope I never lose zest for. What else would incite a fifty-something woman to hurl herself around someone's front yard in pitch darkness? What other occasion could transform giggling girls into fear-soaked ninnies? After all, what other excuse can one have to wallow in total and unashamed self-indulgence if it isn't a birthday?

28 When the Cowhide Dies

There were six people shifting their feet and peeking around the guy in front of them to see what in the world was holding up the line. It was me; my arm submerged elbow-deep into my purse as I grappled for change. Not to make correct change, but to pay my bill.

"I need to buy a new wallet," I said too cheerfully to the checkout person. "My snap won't stay closed and the change always ends up in the bottom of my purse." A nervous titter escaped from my mouth.

It was time to face facts. I did need a new wallet. After eight years of dedicated service, two snap replacements, and numerous seam repairs, it was time to shoot the old cow leather.

Buying a replacement wouldn't come easily. Not that I have trouble spending money. May it never be! In fact, that's why this good ol' gal was about worn out. But she had faithfully guarded remnants of the past eight years: school photos of my boys, important phone numbers, activity passes, insurance cards, my winning half of a one dollar bill, lucky pennies, dry cleaning stubs, lies about my weight, and numerous other treasures that tell my story.

"You've served me well, ol' Gal," I told her gently while stroking the familiar worn leather.

And so the hunt began.

I hadn't looked at wallets for such a long time, I wasn't sure what my choices would be. I only had a few criteria: 1) I needed to get rid of excess baggage so a mid-size would do; 2) I also wanted a hearty size coin purse that would open wide for easy viewing or none at all so I could buy a separate coin purse; 3) most importantly, my new wallet needed to feel good.

You see, I grew up on a small farm around horses and harnesses; saddles, bridles, and reins... each harboring its own comfortable feel and fragrance. Eau de saddle soap being rubbed into leather can be as intoxicating to me as a splash of Giorgio.

So with a bit of nostalgia in my purse and heart, I took off for store number one.

"Can I help you?" a cheery voice asked.

"Yes. I need a new wallet."

"Well, let me show you what we have," she said. She leaned under the counter, then reappeared with a plastic bin stuffed with neat rows of wallets.

My eye went to a long, skinny oxblood one. Perhaps I could go for a new lifestyle. I was convinced that any woman who carried an oxblood wallet (that, of course, match her penny loafers) is an ex-cheerleader and now the wife of a rich man. Naah. My friends would know better. No oxblood.

It was easy to cast aside another 75 percent of the choices just by scanning the case. They weren't natural cattle colors.

Yes, the serious search would be amongst the browns. After all, Brown was my maiden name.

One more eliminating factor became the stingy use of leather. Many wallets looked good on the outside but once open revealed a heavy dose of that shiny material that always wears out after a few months.

"How about...?"

"No," I interrupted. "That's too large... small... long... wide... too much like my old one." But mostly I found myself saying, "It just doesn't feel good. It's too stiff... dry... bumpy."

The closest I came to success that trip was wishing "this wallet had that wallet's credit card holder." I expressed my gratitude to the clerk for her assistance and tabled the search for another day.

After dozens of more episodes throughout nine months and an approximate twenty-mile radius, I was beginning to question my criteria. Maybe I needed to compromise. Maybe I should design one and get it crafted. Maybe I should just carry my gear in a plastic bag.

After one final embarrassing mishap with my old faithful wallet, I couldn't take it any more. I decided to go back to the first store I shopped in because it had the largest selection and I was going to buy a wallet.

Armed with a wad of money and determination, I approached the counter. "I am here to buy a wallet and I am not leaving until I do."

Wallets flew left and right. Many were ruled out for the usual reasons; some were set aside to consider on my second go-through; time passed by. After fifty-five minutes it became apparent I wasn't going to love my new wallet. I was going to have to settle for it.

Just when the outlook was darkest, the clerk, sighing and brushing aside an invisible hair from her forehead, reached under the counter one last time. "These aren't actually wallets," she said, "they're passport holders. But some of them might feel good and serve the purpose."

I eyed one with a boxy shape. It was brown. I picked it up. It felt very good. I opened it. It was leather lined. It had a place for credit cards, dollar bills, pictures, and a see-through slot for my driver's license. It smelled good.

I whipped out one of my business cards. It fit perfectly behind the other see-through slot. It didn't have a coin purse. I could pick up one later.

It fit my purse, my hand, my budget, and my nostalgic marriage to leather.

It made the sales lady very happy that I liked it.

That night I made the move, discarding old things out of my wallet. Decisions such as whether to throw away a gum wrapper with a phone number but no name on it can be exhausting. The physical act of letting that old leather go was even more difficult.

But the anticipation of all that my wallet would live through—upcoming events, secrets, I.D. proofing, brag booking, loaning, and storing—got our relationship off on the right foot.

"Well, girl, welcome to my world."

29 Just Hangin' Out With the Girls

*T*he woman plopped her overflowing wicker basket on the ground next to the clothesline pole. The old pillowcase-turned-clothespin-holder hung at arm's length to her right. Dipping her hand into the make-shift bag, she rummaged for the familiar feel of a clothespin with a spring. A spare clothespin was always clipped to her apron, just in case.

T-shirts topped the mound of damp clothes. Picking one up by the bottom edge, she snapped it in the air and then hung it. T-shirts, then socks, then underwear. Always in that order; filling the back line.

Sheets would soon wave from the front line, right after she squished them through the wringer. Drying-time depended on the breeze.

Toward the end of the day, she gathered the white billow in her arms and drew the bundle to her chest. Nuzzling her nose into the folds, she deeply inhaled the captured freshness.

Ah, yes, images of yesteryear.

Or perhaps yesterday, except for the wringer. You see, I am a third-generation flap-'n-snapper, hang-'n-dryer. There is simply no product available that captures the essence of Mother Nature like damp clothes on the line, no matter what the ads say. Once you try hanging out, you're hooked. I promise.

Of course nothing good comes without risk. It might rain; a whirling dust storm might attack; strong breezes can loosen material from the clothespin's grip, sending your dainties flying. A multitude of irritating things can happen.

Another line-drying danger is bird bombs, especially if the birds have been eating blueberries. But number one on my list is, without a doubt, the most humiliating: a lapse of memory whereby I hang the article inside out, thereby announcing my size to every dog-walker in the neighborhood.

And yet, the risk is worth it. There's something wonderfully satisfying and earthy about this meticulous task. Comforting.

I've had interesting conversations with other women who like to hang out. We're quite a dedicated and eclectic bunch.

We all use wooden clothespins. Now I must admit to owning several plastic clip ones, but I only use them in an emergency or if I'm afraid the wood might stain a particular type of material. Unlike Grandma, I have more choices, including the dryer, should weather not cooperate.

But hanging out is for me a welcome hereditary thing (as opposed to some of the unwelcome things, like large hips). Weather never stopped Mom. She hung out on nice, and sometimes questionable, days, as did her mother. I remember following Grandma down into The Cave to crank up her ol' ringer washer. The Cave is what she called it, and that is what it looked like. Some called it a storm shelter. It appeared as a grassy swell in the ground with a door. We ran there when the sky turned black, and stored the canned and "put up" preserves and vegetables on shelves.

Building on Grandma's influence, when Mom grew up she became the keeper of her own clothesline. I can still hear her calling me to help. We'd run and race our fingers down the line in an unsnapping frenzy, tossing clothes over our shoulders, trying to beat a storm; sometimes becoming drenched and laughter-filled in the process. Yes, those were days that produced wonderful memories when mother and daughter fought domestic wars together.

Perhaps that's what I love most about hanging out—all the emotions and memories induced by the process. Oh sure, some say hanging out in cold weather will whiten your clothes while others boast about energy efficiency. Some like to organize clothes as they hang them on the line so they don't have to match socks later; others remove the clothing at just the right dampness for ironing.

For me it's mostly just that the world seems right when I'm snapping and clipping, and watching the flapping, and smelling the fragrance while recalling the sweet essence of yesterdays.

30 A Night Out With Explosives

Yesterday was wonderful. Brian was in town for an overnight visit preceding a one-week class for his company. We made a date, just the two of us, because the next morning he and George were going golfing. This way we'd each have a chance for some one-on-one time with our son. Not that we don't all get along, we do. At least most of the time. But I believe special conversation can flow when interjection by one's spouse can be avoided. (Wasn't that incredibly politely stated? Perhaps I stated it because I am usually the, ahem, interjector.)

Our original plan was to see a movie first, then take in a leisurely dinner. When we arrived at the mall and discovered that our film of choice was playing downstairs in the postage-stamp size theater, as opposed to upstairs in the big-as-it-gets-but-still-not-very-big theater, we decided to rearrange our evening. The new theater is so small that even when you're in the back you're in the front and looking straight up. For cheap money, I could tolerate it; for full pay, which could almost buy admission for a full day at Disneyland, no way!

We went back to the car, where, thankfully, we'd left the newspaper containing theater listings. After a quick glance at our watches, we decided to eat first. I was glad of that decision because I don't wait well. I also knew that if I had popcorn first, I wouldn't eat a proper dinner. (Doesn't that sound like I have a health plan?)

We were seated right away at the restaurant. Quietly I went through the salad menu in hopes of lathering up enough will-power to actually order from it. That was my plan. What came out of my mouth was a request for spare ribs and fries. Mmmmm. I'd skip the popcorn, okay?

Just as we were about to receive our food, the manager asked us if we would mind moving because two parties of ten had just arrived and we were at a larger table. Of course we didn't mind, but as an enticer in case we did, he said he'd give us each a piece of Snickers Pie for our trouble.

We catapulted ourselves to the table he recommended and grinned like fools. We sure didn't want to make the nice man feel terrible by denying his generous offer. Wouldn't that have been rude? I've taught my son better manners.

By the time we were done eating, we were both stuffed. We'd have probably each graciously received our piece of pie and taken it home, but since we were going to the theater, it would melt in the car. So we ordered one and split it.

When we arrived at the theater, I nearly had to be rolled down the aisle. Right after I sat down, I had to go to the bathroom. You can only pack so many food items into one body without causing a squeeze to those internal organs. I had time to make it before the movie began if I hurried.

I realized on my way back to the theater that the pie had left me thirsty, so I got in line to order a diet cola. Like Pavlov's dog, I ordered popcorn (extra butter on the top and in the middle because I have a right to die by popcorn fat if I want to) and a large diet cola to wash it down. I couldn't believe what I'd done. Surely I have a subconscious death-by-explosion wish. Time to call the talk shows.

For the record, I didn't finish the popcorn; I took some home for George. Sometimes we have to seek solace in the small victories.

31 The Little Apron That Could

Each of us possess items with no earthly value, but the minute we see them, memories flood our minds. I have many such items (a few too many, George thinks); I keep them in my view. Some comfort me, some make me laugh. They range from rocks to photos.

Recently I lost one of those items; a pocket knife with a green cover, not more than 2-1/2 inches long. Its blade was shaped like a saber, and it was incredibly sharp. The knife belonged to my grandmother, and I loved using it.

I often imagined what Grandma might have sliced, diced, screwed, slit, or stuck with it. George and I used it just before it disappeared. We were on vacation, sliced a beef salami, and then the knife was gone.

Another of my favorite items is a five-inch diameter rock on a pedestal in our living room. Mom fished it out of the bottom of a lake the last time we caught a fish together.

Several months after Mom's death, I went through her belongings. I sifted through her closet, hanger by hanger. Certain events and outings were triggered by familiar dress clothes, and suddenly, there it was: the apron. It's a pinafore type and ties in the back, with one pocket on the right front. It's probably all cotton, but I don't know for sure. Instantly, I was weeping. I could hardly look at it. The pain was too close, instant, and piercing.

You see, Mom loved to entertain, she loved her home, her duties, and her agenda; but most of all, she loved us. She loved doing for us. And she often wore that apron during the doing. The apron seemed to be a beacon flashing reminders that would nevermore be.

The worn apron now hangs on the wall in my office, a silent reminder of time well spent: peeling potatoes; making her specialty pineapple cream pie with meringue; planting pumpkin seeds in her hand-shoveled mounds of rich black earth; running her Electrolux in a complete panic before company arrived; gifting us with country fried chicken, mashed potatoes, corn on the cob (out of the garden, of course), and the best white chicken gravy laced with crunchies from pan drippings that any human ever put to palette.

The apron also elicits memories of her spunk: how she stood up to a shoe salesman who tried to tell her it was our fault her little girl had blisters on her feet; shooting a fox in our basement; driving a delivery truck to Chicago when she was nine months pregnant to help my father's new business stay afloat; becoming a business woman for the first time, after age fifty; and emptying a punch bowl over the head of a blond bombshell who had flirted once too often with my father....

The apron represents hot tea and cold watermelon.

Ironing and wash on the line. Popsicles when we were sick, and Sunday evening popcorn and fresh squeezed lemonade when we were well. It reminds me of the scent of Lilies of the Valley, with which mom slathered herself once a year when Coty released its new batch. It conjures up images of Mom holding her first-born grandson close to her breast and weeping.

And laughter. Endless peals of laughter so quick to pour from her bountiful and overflowing joy-filled spirit.

I thank God for this symbol of motherhood. And, like the knife, should the apron disappear on one of *those* days, although I'll be sad, I know I'll never lose the glorious memories given to me from my "no earthly value," but "all that matters" items.

32 The Pressure of Being Cool

T he day began fairly routinely. I was bombing through the office, wearing yesterday's makeup. A bad habit, I might add, that I swore I was going to stop because I'd heard it increases wrinkles.

I was happy. Grounded. Fairly secure. I think it was mid-week, maybe a day earlier.

An editor across the room said something to me. I couldn't hear her and asked her to repeat it. She waved me over. I knew I was either about to hear a secret or be reamed out.

She said I was invited to a party. I smiled. She said I had been "voted in." It was a party for "cool people." No duds, nerds, or generally uncools allowed.

My heart leapt. Someone thought I was cool. Obviously more than one person had voted for me, so maybe three or four people thought I was cool. It must be true.

I was warned: "Do not let anybody know about this. Anybody. We don't want uncool people to find out about it and show up."

I was informed of time and date, which was moved three times within fifteen seconds. Obviously, there was a burning hunger for this party to begin. A group of women looking for some relaxed fun.

I couldn't wait to tell my family. I started dragging clothes out of my closet in search of the "coolest" outfit I owned, just to make sure I'd be ready.

Swell. I owned one acceptable outfit and it was a size I hadn't fit into for three years.

Oh well, don't worry, I told myself. You must dress cool enough or you wouldn't have been voted in. Maybe just the fact my earrings usually don't match comes off as eclectic or artsy or something.

My husband, instead of swooping me into his arms and swirling me around, frowned and said: "You were voted in? What kind of party is this going to be?"

"All girls."

For days, I was drawn to every mirror I passed like my teenage son who flexed his biceps at every mirrored encounter. Sometimes I would stop and search deep into the reflection of my eyes, looking for seeds of coolness.

I had never in my life been "in" with the "cool" group. In high school I was told that if I wanted to be a cheerleader, I would have to be nicer to the cool kids in order to work my way into their crowd.

I told them I was who I was. I was either cool or not. I could not be who I wasn't to be cool. The caption by my picture in my graduating yearbook said, "She would rather sit on a pumpkin and have it all to herself than be crowded on a velvet throne." After spending my youth thinking I'd been slammed, as an adult I discovered this was right out of Walden Pond.

I was not a cheerleader.

The closest I ever came to being cool was being invited to attend the Bra Club in sixth grade. The qualifications for staying a member were simple: Show your bra strap every day. And we were very discreet about disclosure. We met a good six or seven rows back into the corn field that was kitty-corner from school. Of course in the fifties, no one would have thought about not wearing their bra, especially after their mom had to drive them all over the county looking for an actual bra that didn't have any actual cups, just two triangles, because there was no actual goods to put in them.

Now someone, no several, had decided that I was cool and life changed. I had something to live up to. Had I presented something I'm not? They don't really know me. What would happen when they did?

Maybe people thought I was cool because I laugh a lot. What if I couldn't think of anything funny to say? Would I be voted out after one meeting?

I told Bret about my party. We have like minds, and I thought he would get a huge charge out of his mom being cool. I received a lecture about how I never let him and Brian judge about the coolness (or lack thereof) of others.

He reminded me of my long-windedness on this topic, and how he had come to believe it. He wondered aloud what happened to Mom.

It was forty-five minutes until party time. At 7:30 A.M. I made my snackie to pass. I still had to take a shower and decide what to wear. I closed my eyes; the pressure was tremendous.

Maybe I should stay home, I thought.

No! Bret's words twirled in my conscience. I would go and be myself! I would live or die (or be voted out) for who I was. I would wear very shiny lip gloss and large earrings that always gave me confidence. I would be no more or no less than who I was. Period.

I have decided what I taught my boys about judging is good and true and right. I thank the Lord that He always remembers to remind me about what I forget. Now that's really cool.

33 A Study in Human Nature

I didn't have a clue what I was in for. I'd volunteered to collect contributions for Tag Day for Family Service DuPage, a non-profit organization that offers a wide range of services from Big Brothers, Big Sisters to temporary housing for the elderly.

I was excited about helping further the work of a good cause; I looked forward to all the people I'd meet and the conversations we'd have, not to mention all the money I'd collect.

"How'd you do?" I asked, approaching the not-so-smiling face of the person I was replacing.

She gestured by shaking the tin receptacle in her hand. Coins clattered, and she acted like the weight of them might tip her over. Being a first-time tagger, I assumed this was a positive response to my question.

"Good thing you wore your winter coat," she said flatly as she passed me without another word and disappeared into the parking lot. Curious. I was sure I'd be shedding my wool bulk within a few minutes. After all, it was April.

I settled my feet directly over where I'd seen hers

planted, assuming this was the official spot. Checking my pocket for the tags to pass out to contributors, I found them secured with a rubber band. As I was positioning myself to what I thought would be an appropriate pose, a body flashed by. I had missed my first giver. Better pay attention and be ready for the next smiling (I was sure each would be) face. I knew business would be snappy. My post was just outside the doorway to a local grocery store, and it was Saturday. Two hours of volunteer time would pass quickly.

Before I could finish that thought, the electronic doors swung open, and out rolled a grocery cart piled high with bags. I readied my can and waited for the person pushing the cart to become visible. The cart seemed to be picking up a head of steam, and before I could say "Hi," a woman raced by, hiding behind her bags. I had missed possibility number two.

I was determined to make eye contact with the next person, and I did. As I held his eyes captive, I reached out with my can and started to open my mouth.

"I gave on the way in. How many times do I have to give?" He pulled up his jacket collar and stomped off.

I decided to pay closer attention to those entering. Just my luck, someone was coming my way.

"Hello. Would you like to make a contribution to...."

"Don't have any change. Get you on the way out." Guess I'd have to start memorizing who gives on the way in and who will get me on the way out.

A smartly dressed elderly lady exited from the store, one arm clutching a brown bag, the other outstretched towards me. The sunlight glistened off the silver extended from her fingers. She plunked in her coins. A beginning at last.

"Thank you very much," I said smiling. "Let me give you a tag." I reached into my pocket and tried to jostle one loose from the rubber band. Unsuccessful, I pried the whole packet from my pocket. The rubber band popped off and they spilled out all over the ground, blowing everywhere. I grabbed one and handed it to my generous giver, then started scurrying to retrieve the rest. At least five people passed while I was gathering.

Once I gained my composure, the next several shoppers contributed to the cause. I relaxed my guard. Mistake. I was confronted by a man wearing a business suit and an angry face.

"I'm sick and tired of being bugged for weeks at every corner in this town. How many times can you people beg for money? Can't a man get on the train or buy a loaf of bread without someone's donation can in their face?" He stormed into the store. I checked my watch. A whopping ninety-three minutes of my post was left. Just two quick hours, huh? The cold air started settling in.

During the next ninety-three minutes many shoppers treated me as if I were invisible. I even saw one lady working so hard at trying not to notice me, she walked into the corner of the building. It was the first time I could relate, in a very small way, to what it must feel like to be down and out.

But it was an insightful experience I would do again. In fact I have. I look upon the experience as an adventure, a study of human nature. Most of the shoppers were kind and generous. Some of those who chose not to contribute, looked straight at me, smiled, and said "No thanks." There's dignity in that.

Of course, no one should feel obligated to put something into a donation can. Who knows what other charities people might support? Who knows what financial position one might be in on any given day? Who knows?

Yes, it was one of those days that contained many lessons. One of those days when life took some strange twists and turns, and occasionally rammed a brick wall, all because of little ol' me.

<u>34</u>   Modern *In*conveniences

Recently I tried to use my new phone credit card to make a call from Indiana to my answering machine in Illinois to retrieve any business messages.

I dialed the code for my carrier, then dialed zero plus the phone number. This activates a signal that lets you know when it's time to punch in your card number. In this case, the card number is our home phone number, sans area code, plus a personal identification number (PIN) printed on the front of the card. The card I'd never used before.

At the sound of the tone, I punched in my string of numbers. A recording came on, asking me to punch in my PIN, which I'd already done, but I did it again.

Another recording came on announcing that this was an invalid number, to please hang up and dial the number again. Once again, I had to begin by pushing the right code to get my carrier, then the number I was calling, then my string of credit card numbers, only to be caught in the same loop.

Okay, so maybe even though my area code wasn't on the

card, maybe I was supposed to punch it in. I hung up, did the entire series again, and this time used my area code, only to get another recording. I hung up and dialed the operator.

I explained my dilemma. She asked me what number I was calling; I told her. She asked me what my card number was; I told her. She said I wasn't reading my PIN correctly. I asked her how many ways are there to read three digits? She replied that I must be reading the wrong spot on my card. I took a deep breath and said, "It says P-I-N on my card, and these are the numbers that follow it."

She put me on hold for a very long time and another person came on. I started from the beginning.

He said that I must have asked the company not to print my PIN on the card, in which case they would have sent me a separate mailing telling me my secret code.

I told him there was no such request, and no such mailing. I was talking through my teeth by this time. He was snipping and talking down to me, which I did not appreciate.

We went through the PIN again and he asked me to hold on while he checked something. After a v-e-r-y long hold he came back on and said I was missing a number. The PIN is supposed to be four digits long and I only had three. Since my first three were correct, the laser printer must not have printed the last number.

"Okay, so what is it?"

"I can't tell you."

"Excuse me?"

"I cannot tell you."

"Why?"

"Because how do I know if this is really you? It's a security measure."

"So how can I ever use my card?"

"Hold on please."

Before I could scream, "don't put me on hold," I was there. After another very long time, he came back on and said he would call my answering machine and leave the number. I could retrieve it with the rest of my messages.

"You mean I now have to make a long distance call from someone else's phone so I can get my credit card number before using my credit card to return calls from my answering machine?"

"Yes."

"Why should I have to pay for the phone company's mistake?"

"Wouldn't you rather pay for one extra call than have us give your number to a thief and have them rack up hundreds of dollars of calls?"

"I'd rather not pay for your mistake. Period."

There was no budging him. This was my only choice.

"Fine."

"Hold on, please, while I call your home." Before I could say, "Don't put me on hold again, call me back!" I was on hold. After a very long time he came back and told me he couldn't leave a message because a fax machine answered. I asked him what number he was dialing and he gave me my business number, instead of my home number, which I asked for.

"Oh. Hold on."

Finally, f-i-n-a-l-l-y, he came on and said my answering machine hadn't come on, but he'd left my number with my husband.

"Interesting," I said. "He isn't home."

"Well someone answered your phone and said they were Mr. Baumbich and I left them the message."

My heart skipped a couple of beats before I remembered that Brian was due to come home that day. He must have answered the phone. If not, the thief who was now in my home, posing as my husband, could now conveniently make zillions of long-distance calls from anywhere in the cosmos using *my* number, which I would be unable to use until I was able to track *him* down.

"Will you send me a new card?" I asked.

"Why? You'll never forget the number now."

"Because it should be right. And how do I know it was just the laser printing and that in fact the magnetic strip isn't also bad? Then it won't work in the automatic phones where you just stick your card in."

"I'm sure that isn't the case," he said.

"Send me a new one anyway," I demanded. I had been on the phone for thirty-two minutes! I was exhausted.

I was about to unload the scenario on a friend but was stopped short by her news that her husband's cancer had returned. Funny what a good dose of perspective can do.

"How are you?" she asked. "You look a little tired."

"I'm fine. Just fine."

35 Cruisin' through Life

Throughout my life, cars have made a definite impression. Perhaps it isn't the cars, but the memories that surround them. Significant memories that are time-stamped by a specific auto.

The first car was Nellie Bell, a Plymouth we had when I was in fifth grade. She had that old-car smell and faithfully delivered us to the Riverview amusement park every year.

Nellie Bell was difficult to start. The engine would be cranking and cranking and Mom would be pumping and pumping on the gas peddle, pleading, "Come on, Nellie Bell!" And finally Nellie Bell would cough and sputter to life.

"Good girl," Mom would say as she patted the dash board. And we kids would sit in the back seat and cheer. I realize now that the Nellie and Nellie duo (my mom's name was Nellie) taught me a lot about faith. We always wondered if Nellie Bell would start; always acted like she would; and always cheered when she did.

Next up in my walk through automobile memory lane

comes the crystallized vision of the first of two Chevrolets that mattered. It belonged to Grandpa Landers. Probably circa late 1940s. It was a low-riding, maroon and black, sort of puffy-at-the-corners beauty that never went more than thirty miles per hour, slowly weaving its way across the countryside because Grandpa needed to absorb the scenery.

A little visor-type thing stuck out above the windshield, giving the car a mysterious look. Grandpa's ever-present, tilted-down, wide-brim hat matched the car perfectly. And the car was always filled with smoke, because Grandpa was. Sometimes he let me light 'em up for him when no one was looking.

Grandpa was a horse trading, genuine, capital "G" Grandpa who loved babysitting us. He always told Grandma and Mom we never gave him any trouble, which we didn't because he never gave us any rules.

That car and Grandpa symbolized finding the best in everyone and every path. Taking your time. Drinking in God's wonderful bounty.

My next auto of importance was the brand new, powder blue Ford wagon my dad totaled. The car rolled and hit a telephone pole and Dad lived to tell about it. It was a scary and blessed day and was certainly a "yes" vote for the old, durable wagons. That evening sitting around the kitchen table we realized life is fragile.

That family wagon was a far cry from the first of our "loaded" cars that followed, cars that displayed our celebration of life.

Loaded Buick Electras. Three in a row. Power everything. (We're talking late 50s, early 60s here.) They covered my eighth grade field trip to Abraham Lincoln Land, speedball trips to high school when I'd missed the bus, shopping for prom dresses in Elgin at Joseph Spiess Company, and much more.

And then... I got my very own powder blue, 1957, two-door hardtop Chevrolet! A world away from Grandpa's Chevy, but what a Chevy it was! (And wouldn't I give my eye teeth to park it's shiny little backside in my driveway today!)

I earned money for that prize by being a very bad waitress (not intentionally) and working in the office of my dad's tool and die company in the summer.

Driving to Wheaton Central High School every day was a necessity because in 1963, the year I graduated, we attended half-day sessions due to overcrowding. The other half of the day I and my Chevy tooled out to Roberts Beauty School so I could learn how to be a hairdresser, which I never became.

Sandwiched in with all the coolness of my '57 Chevy was Larry's black, 1959 Ford Starliner with glass packs, a big engine, expensive tires, a great stereo (the tunes always went straight through our hearts), a red velvet throw pillow for the back window and a matching red velvet stick shift cover that I made. The best thing that car had, though, was Larry.

I don't remember what it did the half-mile in, but I do remember my parents hated that... that... hot-looking, very fast, black and red baby trap. But we were much more innocent than they thought we were.

I'd say Larry was my first real love, and he rumbled into my life in genuine style.

There's a big leap between the sweet memories of the Starliner and the next vehicle that stands out in my mind; perhaps that's because there was a four-year marriage (not to Larry) in that time span that didn't survive. But the next memorable auto came at the end of that marriage.

The brand-new, white 1967 Ford Falcon was more than a car to get me places; it symbolized my independence. I bought it, without any assistance. Miraculously, I didn't get ripped off. In fact, I struck a good deal! I even did all the financing by myself!

I was still driving that car when the green, 1966 Buick Wildcat rolled into my life with a 6'2" man named George behind the wheel. It certainly wasn't a car like Larry's. But I was older, wiser, more mature. George and I began our married life together with that car.

Our first home, the one we still live in, has a two-car garage. There those cars sat, side by side: a no-frills Falcon and a far-roomier but really no-frills Wildcat, except for its big engine.

The cars we have gone through since as a no-frills, married couple have been nothing short of boring, but basically reliable. The most exciting thing we've ever splurged for is power windows. (Okay. Our newest car, a white, 1985 Buick Century, has a lighted vanity mirror on the passenger-side visor, if that counts.)

Somehow we've missed needing the mid-life red sports car, although I did go through a phase of wanting a 4 x 4 pickup truck, which my son actually got and I occasionally borrowed to go on devil-may-care, rip-through-the-gears, treks to KMart. But basically we're pretty boring, just like our cars.

Oh, our boys have given us a series of thrills with some of their $100 rusted-out bombers that caused more trouble than one could possibly dream. But then, those automobile memories and the days they churn up really belong to them, don't they?

36 Stop, Thief, You Stole My Perky Face!

George and I were getting ready for vacation. We were more excited than usual because we were going to see Bret's newly-purchased home. His first. A place he was very proud of and anxious to share with his parents.

Bret lives in Albuquerque, New Mexico, as does my father and his wife. Lord knows, I'd need the proper attire and face creams when venturing into the Southwest. A new hat (please, please keep any more of those dreaded brown age spots from sprouting) was in order. We're not talking designer variety; we're talking cover the top of the head to prevent heat stroke and an extra long bill to keep me shaded. So I was off to KMart, where I found the perfect hat.

It was the only one of its kind and it was pink; the kind of pink that gave my face a rosy glow. Yes! It had an extra long and extra wide bill starting from near the back of the head to shield my delicate (and old unelasticized) skin. It was mine and on sale. I bought it.

Our first day in Albuquerque, I donned my new hat. People noticed it and complimented me on not only its color and style, but also on how perky and swell it looked on my head. I loved my new hat and saw not another like it.

The day before we were to return home, Dad and Wendy and George and I were going to hit the flea market one last time. I strapped on my fanny pack that holds my water bottle (it's very dry in New Mexico and I am constantly sipping and applying lip gloss) and searched for my wonderful pink hat, which was missing. I tore the place apart.

Then it occurred to me. I'd left my hat in Old Town, where I'd been on an all-day shopping excursion the day before. I just knew it was in the T-shirt shop.

Yes, I had undoubtedly left my hat in that store. I convinced everyone that we needed to stop by there, I'd run in and get my hat, then we'd be off to the flea market.

Just as we were pulling up in front of the store, a lady stepped off the curb, right from in front of the T-shirt shop. She was chatting with two other women, laughing, looking both ways. She was wearing my hat.

Before I could open my mouth, Wendy said, "There's your hat, Char. That woman is wearing your hat!"

"I was just thinking that!"

"Go get it from her," Dad said.

"Yeah," George chimed in.

"I can't just say, 'Give me my hat' to a total stranger. I'd have no way of proving it's mine. Besides, maybe it isn't. Maybe mine is still in the store. Let me out, Dad, please." I was in the back seat of a two-door car. I finally unfolded myself and had to take the usual moment to shake out the mid-life cramps that come following strenuous activities like sitting for more than five minutes.

Sure enough, my hat was not in the store. The sales person said she hadn't seen it, but looked particularly guilty. You know that look: tight lips, lack of eye contact. I ran back out into the street, but my pink hat and the head it was on had disappeared. Everyone in the car said, "Let's go track her down."

"I'd have no way to prove it was mine," I repeated. "No identifying mark. No name tag. And it's possible someone else bought a hat just like it at KMart and just happened to be wearing it at that particular moment right in front of the store where my exact same one disappeared."

"I haven't seen a hat like that. Ever," Wendy said. "In fact, it was so unusual I was going to ask you to buy me one when you got back to Chicago. It had such a wonderful brim."

"I know. It was the only one I ever saw like it," I lamented.

There is no moral to this story. I am convinced that woman found my hat in that store and put it on her head.

Of course she didn't look nearly as wonderful as I did in it. No, she looked more like a thief. But was she?

What would you have done? Write me if it's brilliant. And if you're wearing a pink hat you found in a T-shirt store in Old Town Albuquerque, please enclose it. I'll be ever so happy. My face hasn't looked as perky since.

37 Spring Sprout Sightings

Folks down Capistrano way enjoy the coming of the swallows. The Midwesterners' version of this annual pilgrimage is quite different, but then so are Midwesterners. One might refer to our "moment" as the coming out of legs. One day, one of those glorious spring days, without announcement, on cue, everywhere you look, legs appear that haven't been seen all winter.

One bright, sunny spring morning I stopped at a fast food chain for a diet cola (yes, for breakfast), and there in line was the first pair I'd seen that year. They were sprouting from a chunky ten-year-old and were as white as the driven snow, exploding out of his shorts like stuffed sausages. He had obviously found those shorts crammed in the back of a drawer and was unaware he had grown one full size.

Well, I started my pop-sipping drive and, within one-half mile from the first sighting, the second pair appeared. This time they were attached to a male jogger with swishing black satiny shorts. They were running as though happily exclaiming freedom from those cumbersome sweats that had clung to them all winter.

During my lunch hour in the park, I saw Them. The first bronzed pair, joined to a lanky young woman who had obviously planned and waited like an expectant mother for this day. The lack of jiggle about her thighs made it clear she hadn't acquired this look without dedication to the grunt-and-bend bandwagon. I was envious.

Not having jumped on the bandwagon, or any other exercise equipment, I vowed my legs weren't going to show all summer. I was slightly depressed all through work.

When my teenager arrived home after school, he banged his books down on the kitchen table and leaped up the stairs two at a time toward his room. After a short while, a stranger's legs appeared. I wouldn't have recognized my own son's legs in a leg line-up. Over the winter hair had incubated under his jeans. Lots of it.

Before the day was over, six more pairs had been sighted. They had either appeared through my front window, flashed by me on a bike as I walked the dog, or were seemingly protruding from my husband's abdomen while his bent-over body turned the soil in the garden.

It was officially official. Spring had sprung by sprouting legs.

38 The Plunge

"**P**ush me as hard as you can, Dad!" came a voice from the depths of a bundled-from-head-to-toe child. He hollered this directive over his shoulder as his father squatted behind the red disk sled. "Push me really fast!"

My backyard overlooks the park across the street where this neighborhood father and son played. I stood silently scratching Butch behind the ears, remembering yesterdays.

Though the days of bundling my own children are decades behind me, I could still almost reach out and pat my own rosy-cheeked sons that we corralled at dusk from the small hills that surround the wooded area by our home. Yes, I could almost see them, through time and my blurred vision, running as fast as possible with so many layers on their legs. Laughing.

"Watch this!"

"No fair!"

"You got two turns!"

Belly-flopping onto their blade sleds and whisking into the darkness. Hurling themselves into the drifts. Arms and legs flailing. Leaving imprints of angels behind them. Surrounding them. Secretly guarding them, I always hoped.

"Mom, come give me a shove!"

How many times did I send them spinning, twirling, skittering down a hill? How many times did I wait at the bottom of the swiftest of slides, holding my breath?

How many nights did I wait to hear the sound of their key slide into the keyhole just before curfew, or long after?

How many years has it been since I watched them plunge into manhood?

"Push me as hard as you can, Dad! Push me really fast!" the neighbor child repeats, snapping me out of yesteryear and back into this day. This day of remembrance.

If only the small boy knew how hard his father had to work at not holding him back. And then to let him go. Down the slide. Down the hill. Into life without him.

39 The Good, the Bad, the Geezer

This past May, George and I attended the college graduation of our baby. Although Brian actually finished school in November, Winona State University has only one ceremony a year. And since Brian is gainfully employed (Yippee! Yippee!) in Winona, and has become a Minnesota resident, we would be visiting his new home. Amazing.

On the way, I pondered how fulfilled I am, as wife, mother, writer, and woman. So much behind me, with so many days to look forward to, God willing. And I'm not even fifty years old yet. George and I are young empty-nesters and it feels good. Satisfying.

I pulled down the visor mirror only to slam back up the reality of crows feet and jowls. It's easier to feel young when you're not looking in a mirror.

It was a beautiful Minnesota day and the graduation was nice. There were over one thousand in Brian's class, and they read each person's name. Each graduate had his or her chance to walk across the stage and be acknowledged. I thought about how our names are recorded in God's book and was moved by the uniqueness of each person in that room, whether receiving a diploma, or watching a loved one graduate. So much hard work. So many hopes. So many dreams.

So much debt!

Evening delivered an opportunity for us to see Brian in a new light. A few of his friends threw a lawn party for the graduates. They all had wonderful senses of humor, conversation was lively, and they accepted our presence at the party with a warm welcome, making us feel like very cool parents. Very cool parents who left long before the party was over to hit the sack because we were tired, and, after all, parents.

The next morning George and Brian went golfing and left me to do some serious shopping. That evening we took a consensus and decided we'd dine out, then go to the movies. Us cool-and-young-people, our son, and several of his friends.

Since I was in charge of the money this trip, I purchased the tickets at the window.

"Three adults for *Maverick*," I said. About the time the ticket person was sliding the tickets toward me, I heard George say, "No! Two adults and one senior."

"Right." I laughed and wagged my head at the ticket person.

"No, I'm serious. I just noticed the sign says their senior rate begins at fifty-five."

Save-a-buck George was thrilled to get a discount; I was mortified and quickly sliding into a depression.

"Oh my gosh, I'm married to a senior." Me, the cool,

young, fascinating wife of a *senior*. I tried to distract myself with popcorn and a large diet cola, but even that didn't work. I missed half the dialogue in the show while fretting over this new discovery. George sat grinning from ear to ear like a happy old geezer.

"For better or for worse, for richer or for poorer, in sickness and in health, till death do us part." Aha! The loophole surfaces. "For senior" is never once mentioned!

Then I thought of my widowed friend. How she would embrace the opportunity to again pay for that love of her life—even at a senior discount.

Dear Lord, may George and I pay senior admittance together as Geezer and Geezette for many years to come.

40 All Wrapped Up and No Place to Go

I was sitting in front of my television munching a bag of chips when the phone rang. It was an old friend calling to tell me about a story idea of his.

"Uhuh... uhuh," I interjected as he rattled on about a new body wrapping place that promised to shrink your body without dieting. He had my attention for sure when he got to THAT part. Can you say, "How fast can you speed dial?"

The owner of the month-old franchise, whom I shall refer to as the Potential Miracle Worker (PMW), was extremely enthusiastic about revealing the concept and benefits of the procedure.

She spelled out their two guarantees.

1) Women will lose from six to sixteen accumulated inches in their first wrap; men will lose at least four.

2) The inches will stay off as long as you maintain your weight.

"It is a safe and effective method of losing inches from the right places permanently in only seventy minutes. When I heard about it, I thought it sounded too good to be true," she said. *Exactly*, I thought.

"You can have the buns of a twenty-year old," she quipped.

"How soon can I arrange an appointment for myself and how much does it cost?" She had found my vulnerability, and it would cost $45. She also told me to allow about two-and-a-half hours.

We continued talking while I tried to understand exactly what it was I would lose. Toxins. I would lose toxins that would be extracted, or wrung out, or something.

"How did I get them?" I asked.

She explained that they came from pollution, stress, smoking, injuries, drinking, salt, and sugar. *In other words, just waking up in the morning*, I thought.

She explained the cellulite circle to me (which includes toxins). I was familiar with that dirty word—*cellulite*. But I didn't know that bands of them circled their wagons and captured toxins.

Before we hung up, I had learned: I would get a mini face lift; the bandages would be soaked in mineral solution that was 100 percent natural, pH balanced, and pure enough to drink; I could leave on my mummy casing for three days without harmful results, but it would only remain active for seventy minutes; and their special technique would make me lose inches in exactly the right places.

I might even look better than I ever had, she said. How could I wait two days?

Upon my arrival, I was given a short explanation of the franchise's holistic approach. PMW suggested I: eat well, exercise regularly, drink lots of water, get my wraps (instead of taking them)... the usual. They also told me about their product line of supplements and vitamins.

The mineral solution would extract toxins into the bandages, and the rest would be eliminated by my kidneys, PMW said. Enough talk. She took thirteen measurements of parts of my body I don't care to discuss, and The Wrap began.

A body wrap starts at the feet and works up, ". . . lifting, compacting, firming," PMW said. First one leg, then the other. I had a brief flash of hope for my bust line if all those extra cellulite circles got squeezed like an ice cream push-up to the right place.

I stood, or leaned for balance, while the actual wrapping took place. Women wear undergarments and men wear swim trunks under the wrap. The soaked, stretchy bandages were retrieved from something that looked like a large food warmer that might contain hot dogs.

The process was actually swifter than I thought. It was obvious PMW knew what she was doing, especially when she triple wrapped and tugged the cloths snugly around the somewhat larger areas of my body. I now understood the "special technique."

I felt like a spring from a ball point pen. If I bent, surely I would snap right back up. I tested this as PMW had me lift my legs so she could put baggies on my feet to collect the toxins. PMW said the liquid that ends up in the baggies had been scientifically tested and found to be approximately one-third solution, and two-thirds toxins. The thought of splashing around in my own extracted, squeezed-out toxins wasn't appealing. Toxic dumps aren't popular.

Thankfully, I was distracted from entertaining that picture when PMW began to entomb my head. Then, the final step: a nylon sweat suit for my comfort and warmth, as the wrap swiftly cooled.

I could watch TV, exercise, or just hang out, PMW said. What I wanted to do was hide from any mirrors. "Just concentrate on the new you," I mumbled to myself. Don't think about the fact you look like something out of a B movie.

After I was unpeeled and re-measured, PMW told me I had lost an accumulated total of 10-1/2 inches. That's over thirteen measurements, remember.

I forced myself to peek at my not-so-favorite parts, and they actually looked a little tighter. I still wasn't ready to believe in miracles, though. I slipped on my dress.

The ultimate test came the next morning when I donned my jeans. They honestly were looser in the "specially techniqued" areas. Now there was the "bottom" line.

Sorry to say, however, even the "bottom" line isn't what it used to be.

41 A Mind's Ride to Riverview

When you're a kid, some places are bigger than life. For me, Chicago's Riverview was *the* place. The days of Riverview are deep in my heart.

When it was founded in 1904, Riverview was billed as "The World's Largest Amusement Park." And since it closed in 1967, I can not go back and check the accuracy of my memories. But in my heart and mind, it will always reign as King of Thrills.

It was impossible to experience Riverview without strung-together doses of holding your breath or hearing it rip through the air in supersonic high pitch. No regular breathing. Unless you were posed in one of the old-fashioned cars in the photographer's booth; during which time you grinned like a jerk, chomping at the bit for your next non-breathing experience.

For me, the mere word *Riverview* ignites bursts of vivid pictures: my head snapping as rubber bashed into rubber on the Bump-em cars, or the sun shining through a goldfish bowl I won throwing a ping pong ball. (I learned my new pet would have a very short life span.)

I remember colorful hats held on by elastic bands that were snugged under the hairy little chins of funny yet often obscene monkeys who drove miniature race cars you could bet on. And the sight of giant eyes and a drip-like moustache on the mystical monstrous face looming over the Aladdin's Castle always made my pulse pound its way through my skin.

These images are some of the ones that I can capture in words. But when I take a mind's ride on the Bobs, the Paratrooper, or the Shoot-the-Chutes, I feel... clunking, creaking, surely-breaking sounds as my body was, inch-by-inch, elevated skyward... NOT BREATHING... an eyeblink in time when I was motionless... NOT BREATHING... the split second I was hurled off the planet to probably die... SCREAMING SCREAMING SCREAMING.

It's hard for me to talk about Riverview without longing for my extended family. Hardly a year passed when my seven cousins from Indiana didn't ride the rails of the Monon train to Dearborn Station in Chicago for our annual Riverview escapade. We all would screech at the sight of the bridge over the Chicago River because we knew it would be a matter of minutes before another experience—totally unlike yet exactly the same as last year's—would capture us.

Riverview was more than rides: It was a blend of sensations and endless opportunities to test our guts. Sometimes I would be the only one brave enough to venture inside the Palace of Wonders, or, as it was more commonly referred to, the freak show. I have yet to see so many tattoos gathered on one frame as I did at Riverview. And warts... NO BREATHING... I will spare you further horrors.

When you start recollecting memories from your child-hood—those vivid, exciting, innocent days—everyone starts speaking of their favorite places. I can't believe how many people visited Riverview.

Yes, ask anyone who was there what they remembered about Riverview, and the stories leap forth like frogs. Those were, for me at least, the good old days of amusement parks. Today's wooden roller coasters jar the bad vertebrae in my neck; I don't need the water rides to get my pants wet, just a sneeze.

Thank you Lord for days that fill my memory portfolio.

42 High Adventure With Verbs

Sometimes we simply have to go after those dreams God plants in our hearts. So when I received my invitation to the Society of Midland Authors' Annual Awards Dinner, I immediately read it, then set it on my when-I-get-a-minute pile. (Okay, so sometimes God has to elbow me.)

Fortunately (or unfortunately, as you may discern after reading this) the next time I looked at it was twenty-four hours before the response deadline. In my haste, I sent my thirty bucks for my "ticket to be held at the door."

Lest you be impressed that I am a member of the highly honored and well established (founded 1915) Society of Midland Authors, let me assure you that I am not. I received an invitation only because I pay $5 per year to be on their mailing list.

I decided to be a mailing list subscriber after my first visit to one of their sponsored readings. Although the evening provided good food for thought, I also discovered why I wasn't a member of the Society of Midland Authors.

Besides the fact I didn't have mega credits and bylines to my name, I didn't understand half the verbs many of the literary people used.

Not to be excluded, however, I signed up to be on their mailing list so I could attend further gatherings that might help me grow as a writer. Thus my invitation. Scott Turow, author of the best seller, *Presumed Innocent*, was going to be the featured speaker at the dinner. I knew it might be my only chance to hear the author of a best-seller speak.

I inched along with the snarl of 5 P.M. traffic on the Eisenhower Expressway. Thank goodness I wasn't wearing my watch. I had the distinct feeling that the cocktail hour— "6:00 P.M. cash bar"—was passing me by, but it helped not being sure.

My absolute biggest earrings glistened as I checked them numerous times in the rear view mirror. I hide my nerves behind humongous earrings. After all, only confident people would wear earrings large enough to catch a lunker muskie, right?

A number of things started chiseling away at my bravado before I even entered the Drake Hotel. Things such as missing my turn and not knowing how to get off Lake Shore Drive. And waiting for the valet parking line to move forward, only to discover twenty minutes later (bumpkin goes to Chicago) that the line never moves because people in the know jump out of their cars and hand the keys to the valet. I finally followed suit.

Tapping the shoulder of the man in front of me at the key deposit, I asked him if you tipped the driver when he takes the car or when he brings it back. He looked at me—up and down at me—and finally replied with: "Are you here for the weekend?"

"No!" I spat. "And we don't have these kind of parking problems in the suburbs at the Jewel stores."

After whirring myself through the revolving door into

the Drake, I touched one of my earrings to rekindle the magic as I asked where the dinner was. Three sets of directions later, I finally discovered where I was supposed to be.

I dodged into the ladies room and stared at myself in the mirror. "What are you doing here?" I saw and heard the insecure me ask.

"You paid your thirty bucks," the gutsy me answered firmly. "Why not?" And so we entered The Grand Ballroom together.

Massive chandeliers, reporters, photographers, laughter, knowledge, verbs... me. I desperately scanned the room looking for one other person standing alone. Negative. There were only five minutes left of the cocktail hour; so at least, thank goodness, I wouldn't have to wander around much longer. I could be seated. But where?

I asked a polite-looking lady how she knew where to sit. "There's a number on the front of your ticket envelope," she said.

I found a "1" on the front of mine. Surely that couldn't be right. The "1" table was in the front of the room. Right up front. The lights flickered. I was the first person to park at table "1."

Within a minute, the president of the society was headed my way. I recognized him from the last function I attended. I smiled at him and shook my head in hopes of awakening my dangling earrings.

"Hello," he said. He waited patiently while I explained and stammered and stuttered why I was sitting at table number "1," and how I was sure there had been a mistake since I wasn't even a member.

There had been a mistake, he assured me apologetically. This table was for Scott Turow and his guests. The president knew where there was an extra seat, and making it clear he wasn't booting me out, personally escorted me to table "2"—right in front of the podium.

Everyone at table "2" stopped talking as the president of the Society approached with a stranger on his arm. He explained the mix-up in seating and deposited me there. I sat down, adjusted my napkin firmly on my lap and tried to become very small.

I prayed no one would ask me how long I'd been a member. They did. Like their esteemed leader, they waited patiently while I tried to explain, stammer, and stutter out why I was even there at all.

The kind woman seated to my right patted my arm and said I shouldn't feel embarrassed. She said that being a freelance writer was a very responsible and hard job, and she knew that because her daughter was one.

I started to relax. The waiter brought the soup. For the next forty seconds I tried to remember how to swallow gum. I enjoyed my meal, even though I was seated at a table full of judges and winners of the Society of Midland Authors' Annual Awards Dinner.

Turow said he was "... grateful for the miracle of luck and circumstance." (He also has an M.A. from Stanford.) He said, "As writers, we long for our audience. We yearn for the embrace of those we seek to inspire."

There was a point in his well-received speech where he spoke of his beginning, and how he was "exhausted by the demands" he put on himself. I studied his face and wondered if somewhere in that memory bank of his was an exhausting, stimulating, and embarrassing evening like mine.

When I returned home I discovered that the "1" was in the space marked: Number of Tickets. If I hadn't been so nervous, perhaps I'd have saved myself a lot of embarrassment! But then I wouldn't have this story to tell.

43 'Twas the Thirty Days *After* Christmas

Dear First Page of My Journal,

I'm finally ready for Christmas. Cards mailed. Shopping done. Wrapping done. Baking is as done as it's going to get—all two batches of it. House is as clean as it ever gets during the holidays.

This is the first time all season that I've had time to sit and stare at the twinkly lights of my perfectly shaped, fake Christmas tree.

At last I can take a deep breath and know that the holidays will, in spite of my procrastination and disorganization, all come together. This is the good news.

The bad news is, I'm realizing this on January 5.

∼

January 6. I've decided to record the highlights of my day every day from now on so when bad days come I can look through your pages and be reassured that something good or exciting happens at least once every twenty-four hours.

I'm going to start this tomorrow, however, because as our grandfather clock strikes midnight, I find nothing happened today that's worth writing down except this good idea I have about writing things down.

~

January 7. I'd like to make the following announcement, Dear Journal: "I hereby declare myself ready to make good on my New Year's resolution to take charge of my life."

New Year's Day was supposed to be the kickoff for this transformation. But hurling myself on the couch to watch football and eat buttered popcorn with the rest of the family seemed a more giving thing to do than to selfishly isolate myself with celery sticks and devotional books. Besides, I couldn't begin my diet until the last of the Fanny Farmer Candy was gone, so I personally saw to that this morning.

I've spoken to God about the dieting dilemma—for five days running. My self-discipline is at an all-time low, although I'm sure I can chalk much of my lethargy up to sugar blues, P.M.S., and my mid-life crisis. Also, eating tastes so good.

Speaking of eating, I've got to exchange the pair of ten-years-too-small slacks George got me for Christmas.

~

January 8. I'm embarrassed to report that the Christmas lights curled around our evergreen are still popping on at dusk, thanks to the wonders of electrical doodads that turn an ordinary switch into a timer. Seems we're the last twinklers left on our street—except, of course, for the Bradleys, who never take their's down.

Have to tell you, I'm feeling extra clever about buying three packages of slashed-price sale Christmas wrapping paper today for next Christmas. The exhilaration ranks right up there with the high I get when I manage to have dinner cooking in the crock pot by mid-morning. (Yes, Dear Journal, I am easily entertained! And see, something good does happen every day.) Too bad the dirty crock pot sometimes remains on the counter for two days before I wash it. Oh well, who'd ever want to be perfect?

~

January 10. Can't write much. In a rush. Promised myself that today is the day the tree is coming down! I'm beginning to fear if the house received a good shake, the dust would choke us all to death, including the parakeet, the gerbil, and my faithful dog Butch. (Wonder what a gerbil cough sounds like?)

It's not like I haven't been busy! Barb and I had a belated Christmas luncheon yesterday (whoops, oh whoops, dear calorie count). And I exchanged the slacks George gave me for some of those sand-filled weights that Velcro around your limbs. You know, extra calorie burning, extra sweat... extra pain.

~

January 13. I found the key ring I was going to put in Brian's stocking today. Why do I insist on hiding things every year and then forget the secret places? How did I expect to remember something hidden in a filing cabinet under "S"? Do you suppose that meant stocking? Well, at least finding it was a pleasant surprise, unlike the time I hid the chocolate bunny and found the near-white, deformed, one-eyed nightmare lurking behind the Worchestershire sauce in the cabinet above my stove.

~

January 15. Cloudy. Depressing. Tripping over Christmas piles of stuff that need to be boxed. I've gained two pounds and am still five days behind on my devotional reading. Like St. Paul, I wonder why I do the very things I hate... except for eating and day-dreaming which, of course, I seem to love.

And, as you already know, there just isn't time to write stuff down every day. I wish I hadn't made my January 6 promise to "record the highlights of my day every day" in ink because I could have simply erased it now instead of having to live with the falsity of my indelible words.

~

January 17. Let this Christmas forever go down as The Great Underwear Caper. How could I be so wrong about *everyone's* taste in undergarments? I've spent days exchanging my mismatched gifts.

First, I had to exchange the beautiful camisole I bought my niece—get this—for a pair of designer boxer shorts.

Next, Brian, my very own flesh and blood, was sorely disappointed I bought him Jockey Classic Briefs, which, I might add, cost a good buck. He wanted the bikini underwear that comes in a tube.

Worst of all, George snubbed his nose at the cute pair of blush-red, low-rise undies I gave to him "From Santa." He said that "at my age I'm not about to start wearing anything without a fly built into it."

(Lord, thank you for... for... instructing me not to lean on my own understanding. I don't seem to have any.)

~

January 20. The boxes have actually hit the attic. It's amazing how large my house seems with all the decorations down and the furniture put back in place. And I must admit it's nice to have a needle-free post holiday (Yea, fake tree!), although those pesky, prickly little things were at least a six-month reminder that Christmas really did happen.

~

January 24. I received the most beautiful thank you letter from Mary today. She loved, loved, loved the earrings and said they were "really her" and that it was "just like me" to find something that was "so perfect."

You know, every Christmas there seems to be one gift that I get so excited about finding. That one thing that demands the most spectacular bow. But best of all is when it's for someone like Mary whom I know will get all big-eyed and mushy about it.

(Lord, help me to be a good receiver of special gifts. To be wide-eyed and mushy—and to never forget the thank you.)

~

January 30. I just can't bear to part with the last trace of Christmas. The mistletoe still looks so green and inviting... I fear everyone will lose their pucker power until next year if I part with my beloved mistletoe.

My family says the magic wears off mistletoe by the end of January. I bet it lasts at least until Valentine's Day. We'll see.

~

February 1. The dog chewed holes in my sand bag weights yesterday. Maybe February won't be so bad after all.

44 How to Have Your Nails and Chew Them, Too

The other morning my friend Mickey picked me up for breakfast. Normally we meet once a week at a local hangout where everybody knows our name and our diet colas with lime are served without asking. Yes, even for breakfast.

The minute I hopped in the car, I noticed the splint on the index finger of her right hand.

"What happened to your finger?"

"My nail."

"Oh no! Did you rip the whole thing off?"

"No, but it felt like it. I took Butkus (Isn't that a great name for a dog? A big dog who eats their furniture!) out for a walk. I had his chain wrapped around my hand and he decided to bolt. I tried to yank the chain but it squeezed my hand (she does a great demo here, including the face contorted-with-pain) and broke my acrylic. But before it broke,

187

it pulled my nail way back and it kills! Besides, the whole acrylic is loose now and I'm trying to keep it on until I get it fixed. That's why I'm wearing the splint." Aren't vanities wonderful? This is like putting a bandage across your eye to hold on a fake eyelash that's loose.

I felt sorry for Mickey. Talk about a double whammy! A real nail and a fake nail. Of course it's only the fake one that will cost. Real money, too. I know; I wear them. Actually, I don't wear fake nails. My manicurist prefers to call them "a protective coating."

About a year and a half ago, I was visiting with my friend Kim in her floral shop. Next thing I know, I'm showing her how my thumb nail is cracked, down below the quick.

Suddenly, a beautiful redhead leans over, takes a quick look and says, "Why don't you stop in my shop next door? I'll put a protective coating on it until it grows out." Kim vouched for Kathy, said she did good work. I stopped in and made an appointment for a manicure. Might as well treat myself. It's almost my birthday anyway—in five months.

While she applied the protective coating to my thumb nail, I gave her my sordid and sorrowful nail story. How I chew them. How when I don't, they do things like *this*. How I'm spending far too much time trying to make them look presentable because I do a lot of speaking and book signings.

"Would you be interested in a protective coating on all of them? That way they won't break and the polish will stay on." Her voice was smooth as silk and I, of course, found the idea irresistible. I left the store wearing ten perfectly matched, active-length nails. They were shiny and painted the color of Good and Plenty candy; the name of the polish. I was hooked.

For the last fifteen months, I've gone every two weeks for a fill and new polish job. I've heard amazing nail stories in the shop. Some women would clean toilets for a living before they'd give up their nails. I'm not sure I'd go that far, but I'd go far. I remember the days of glue-on glamor and the trouble those things got me in. Talk about humiliating.

I was invited to a gathering of newspaper people at a trendy restaurant in Chicago. I was honored to be invited into this inner sanctum since I was only a freelancer and nervous about looking right. My nails were at an all-time gnaw level, so I picked up some of those glue-on ones. I spent lots of time filing and roughing and polishing and all the things you do so they look natural.

We were eating Italian bread before our meal and crumbs had fallen on the tablecloth around my plate. One of my favorite parts of crusty Italian bread is the crumbs. I dabbed at them with my finger and popped them in my mouth. At the first c-r-u-n-c-h my eyes flew open in shock.

You guessed it. I'd found a new way to chew my nails.

You know, come to think about it, I might wash toilets for a living if I had to. I really might.

45 Whirligig, Whirligig, Take Me Away

My friend Darcy was about to have her first child, and she was ripe with womanhood. Full blossom.

She and I met for lunch one day as close to her due date as we dared. I wanted to give her a baby gift because I didn't know how soon I'd see her after the birth of her child.

I love shopping for baby presents. All the best of expectation wrapped and tucked under a bow, before the reality of poopy diapers, colicky cries, and sleepless nights set in. She didn't know the sex, but she believed it to be a boy. So did I. I entered a shop with that in mind, knowing I shouldn't be cocky about our speculation. God's funny that way.

I meandered from cute little nighties to blankets to stuffed animals. I picked up tiny socks and fluffy rattles and bowls with rabbits on them.

And then I saw it. The perfect gift: a multi-colored whirligig hat. It's a multi-colored beanie with a propeller on the top. I hadn't seen one for years. But, oh, the memories it washed up. Yes, this was the perfect gift for the baby, but especially for my friend.

Lunch conversation was lively, as usual. She'd ordered a palm tree for the baby's room. A fake one, of course, but she was still in shock as to how much they were spending. The bunch of bananas alone was going to set them back a hefty bundle, but they'd decided it was a necessary accessory.

My gift now seemed absolutely perfect. Yes, they'd appreciate the whirligig. It would look swell propped on one of the branches.

Finally it was time to open the gift. As she was untying the ribbon, I held my breath. Every great and wondrous thing about my mothering days consumed me. Every dirty face, every time one of my boys transformed themselves into Superman, or Batman, or whomever they wanted to be. Every fort, every baseball game, every sparkly rock and Lego creation. This hat represented all possibilities.

If people believed it enough and wore this propeller, I'm sure they could fly. With just the right shoes and just the right sidewalk, and on one of their fastest days....

When Darcy pushed back the tissue, she just stared. I'm not sure what she thought it was, even after she'd removed it from the box. Then she began to laugh, twirling the whirligig with her finger. Blowing it. Making it spin. Putting it on her head.

Tears pouring down my face, I tried to explain what the hat symbolized to me. I hoped she'd catch my vision.

I told her about the day three-year-old Bret stood at our front door, covered with mud, wearing an army helmet and a towel for a cape that was pinned around his neck.

"Bret! Look at you!" I said, trying to sound disapproving while holding back a smile.

"I'm not Bret. I'm Superman." And indeed he was. And

I was Superman's mother. Oh, the possibilities! Oh the places in our hearts we'd travel, the memories we'd log.

Whirligig hats hold those powers. I just know it. Maybe I'll buy one for myself and hope that if the wind is just right and I run fast enough, it can take me back in time, just for a little while.

<u>46</u> I'm Alive!

When I check in to drive for senior citizen hot meals, I pick up a map, individual cards concerning special instructions for clients, and, of course, the food.

The directives may vary. "Don't knock, go right in." "Enter on the west side and leave the food on the counter." "Hard of hearing." "Two sacks instead of one." Sometimes, in the more condensed apartments, I might be told, "If she's not home, knock on 235."

One day I received a new route. As I sat in my car studying the cards so I wouldn't miss important cues, one card stood out. It had a huge asterisk and the message, "He is ninety-eight." That's all I needed to dream up various scenarios, the most obvious being that I would be the lucky one to try and deliver meatloaf and mashed potatoes to someone who expired in the night.

When I pulled into the circle drive in front of his home, I was given a peek into his personality. There were lawn ornaments everywhere. Animals, signs, posters, shiny things... It was like a little wonderland and I smiled. I opened the hot container, grabbed the oven mitt, selected one of the foil-covered dishes, and sat it on the car roof. Then I got into the cooler and picked out the paper bag with his name on it. My hands were full by the time I got to the door, but I found a way to knock.

And then I waited.

And then I knocked a little harder.

And then I waited.

And then my heart started racing. I tried to discern my next course of action. Look in the windows? Get to a pay phone (before my car phone days) and call 911? Start screaming for help? Call the hot meals facility?

Just before hyperventilating, I heard a rustling noise and the door began to open. Eek open, ever so slowly. At last a small man appeared with a twinkle in his eyes.

"I'm alive!" he bellowed, as loudly as frailty can manage.

"And no one is happier about that than me," I assured him.

He collected the food from my hands and thanked me. I found myself wishing this was the last stop on my route because I would have liked to chat for awhile with this man who still knew how to make a heart sing. This lively, aged person who had a wonderful sense of humor. This gentle soul who understood that everyone delivering food to his home must worry about the same thing.

"I'm alive!" May I never forget to celebrate that fact and pass on that beatific angel's message.

47 The Un-doing of Lunch

It was a dreary Chicago Monday morning. Temperature around forty degrees. No sun. Mist spitting on everything. It was a great opportunity for a leisurely breakfast with a friend and so I called one at 7:45 A.M. to see if he'd care to join me. He said "Sure!" and I was as happy as a clam, until it began: the pre-menu volleying with his conscience.

He felt compelled to note that after breakfast, he'd spend a twenty-minute workout on his Nordic Track *so he wouldn't feel guilty about eating breakfast.*

Time out! When did eating breakfast become a crime? I've always heard it's the most important meal of the day.

Last week a friend and I did lunch. Privately I celebrated that I didn't have to listen to her usual struggle over what she could or should, or couldn't or shouldn't eat. To my utter surprise, she simply ordered. Perhaps my whining about her personality change since she'd decided to take off some weight finally had an effect.

Unfortunately, during most of our time together she unloaded her dismay about the four-piece chicken dinner she picked up the night before. She lamented how much fat she discovered on the thigh, which she eats first because she likes it least; how she picked some of the breading off, although it was the best part and she hated to think she could never eat it again; how she enjoyed the hush puppies, although they were deep fried and...

The week before, I had lunch with friends who decided on Chinese buffet because of the plethora of vegetables and lack of french fries. The week before this same group had dissected the merits of an Italian buffet according to Bad Guys: fats, sugars, and the like; and Good Guys: carbohydrates and fiber.

I tell you, eating has become a high-stress activity. The statistics of people dying from passive smoke are staggering, but I'd like to see some studies on those of us exposed to health nuts. I bet our blood pressure is escalating simply from *their* diatribes. Passive health-nut syndrome. Somebody check it out.

Don't get me wrong. I believe living a healthy life is not only commendable, but intelligent. And I have no hidden fantasies about the fact that I would be healthier if I dropped some pounds.

But I hope and pray that should I actually begin this process, my mission doesn't mutate so that I become a dangerous and annoying Health Psycho.

In the meantime I will continue to stop the offensive ranklings with my only weapon: Without batting an eye or hesitating a moment, I order a pattymelt. The mere thought that anyone in this day and age would still indulge in that evil delicacy usually causes a silencing gasp. And that's just fine with me.

<u>48</u> Potty Talk for the Romantically Inclined

It was time to redecorate the downstairs bathroom. Actually, it was time to redecorate the entire house, but what we could afford in both money and patience was this four-by-four room. The 60s look just didn't cut it.

"New wallpaper?" George asked.

"No, I want to paint it the same color as the living room. I might put a border around the middle, or the top, or both. We'll see."

"Okay. I'll start stripping the old stuff, then I'll paint. Be done with it in no time."

"No, George. Yes, I want paint, but I also want a new sink and toilet and medicine cabinet and light fixture and towel bar and tissue holder and matching garbage can."

"What's wrong with our old toilet? It still gets the job done."

"It's yellow and I don't want to decorate around it again. I'm sick of yellow. I don't look good in yellow. Yellow makes me look pale. I'd like this bathroom to match the downstairs for a change."

We shopped here and there and everywhere, educating ourselves to possibilities that fit our budget. We couldn't believe the choices and also how much vanities, sinks, and toilets cost! We'd never had to buy a toilet before, and we were stunned. I mean, come on, all it does is flush.

But how do you want it to flush? Button? Handle? Chrome or goldtone? And in what shape do you want the bowl? Round? Elongated?

Basically, we wanted one just like our old one, just not yellow. That, however, was not a possibility. Using nigh on three gallons to flush is no longer politically or environmentally correct. One-point-five gallons. That's all you get to flush your stuff, so it better be do-able. But locating the right toilet was only half the trouble.

Our old vanity no longer came in that same size with a drawer. I needed a drawer! You just can't organize anything without a drawer. After shopping for weeks, I learned that my drawered vanity was an impossible dream unless we went one size larger. "I'm sure that will fit, George, and it has two drawers!"

After endless hours of thrashing and banging and wrestling the new vanity, George emerged from the bathroom and announced that no matter *how* he moved it, he and this size vanity were not going to fit in that bathroom. It was too big, he declared. It would have to go. But I'll never really know because we couldn't both fit in the bathroom at the same time for me to check it myself.

We distracted ourselves by returning the vanity and getting back on the toilet trail until we couldn't stand that anymore and decided to give it all a rest for awhile.

Lickety split, Valentine's Day rolled around, and George

took me out for a nice dinner at a nearby restaurant. When the waitress asked if we'd like dessert, I opened my mouth to say yes, and George said, "Let's go look at toilets instead." Ah, romance.

I browsed in the vanity section. When I came around the corner of the aisle, I stopped dead in my tracks.

There was my Valentine, halfway down the aisle, knee to the ground, arm submerged up to his shoulder in a toilet bowl. He went from one toilet to the next, methodically making his way to the end of the row, cramming his arm into each one.

It just doesn't get much better than this.

"What are you doing?" I shouted more than asked. And truly, I didn't want to know. I disappeared around the end of the aisle trying to imagine what was in his mind. Was he trying to figure out where the stuff goes? What?

As it turns out, that is precisely what he was doing. Exactly how big is the space that a mere one-point-five gallons has to flush without plugging up while making its way around all those loop-the-loops? Important. Very important. My hero, the engineer.

Just when I thought the worst was behind us, the round vs. elongated dilemma resurfaced.

"What have we had, George?"

"I don't know."

"Well, did it look like either one of these? I don't think it did."

"We'll have to go home and see."

"George, I don't want to have to come back here *again*."

He studied my face for a moment and realized that if he asked me to come back again, he was flirting with a major attack of woe.

"We could just sit on them," I said, "and discover for ourselves. I'm sure our bottoms will recognize a good fit."

George made that snort sound he makes with his nose, but looked as though he might go along with the idea.

Putting all vanity aside, I sat my way down the row; as did George. Date night with the Baumbichs! We nearly cheered when the selection and purchase were made. (We're roundies, in case you're wondering). We could barely wait to install our new white beauty.

And can you imagine the thrill of flushing that puppy for the first time? We were nearly breathless as George pushed our chrome-choice handle.

No more swirling and twirling. No more spinning and rising and tornadoing its way down the tube. Whoosh! That's what you get when you're politically and environmentally correct.

So stop by and see our beautiful white appliance (for lack of a better word) and blue rug with matching tank top and purple tissue box and garbage can and liquid soap pump with matching purple guest towel. All I need now is to frame the picture I've selected and shop for the border.

Oh, if you stop by and we're not home, it's because we've decided to redecorate the upstairs bathroom. You can probably find us in aisle seven. That would be us, lounging in the tubs to see how they fit.

49 *Future* Mothers of the Groom Wear Radar and Keep Their Eyes Peeled

One blessing of being the mother of boys is that one day most of them will end up with a girl. You will finally have a family member who doesn't ask you why you need new lip gloss, or why you are crying *again*, or why you talk on the phone so much. (Okay, so Butch doesn't ask those questions either, and neither does my parakeet, but I have to scoop their poop, and that loses them lots of points.)

Or at least you hope you acquire a daughter-in-law. Or sometimes you hope you do, but please, please, oh please God, not this one! Or, God, if it is this one, help me remember that taste in clothes, entertainment, and annoying habits are not something by which to judge a person— nor, yippie skippie, are they hereditary. But that those gorgeous eyes and great hair and long legs (that I covet) are, and wouldn't they look swell on my grandkids?

Over the years my boys have been involved with an eclectic assortment of young ladies. The lovelies have worn hair of gold and hair of raven—and one had hair of many colors. There have been shy ones and noisy ones and those who didn't speak my language. Some I never met and some I wished I never had. Some sang in the choir and some arm wrestled, others wrestled in a big pool of JELL-O. (Okay, so it was the same person who did the unique and varied kinds of wrestling, but she made awesome mashed potatoes. And aren't we to find the good in everyone?)

Some have slipped right into my life and others scared me out of my wits, causing me to lose my beauty sleep and pray like a banshee. "Yes, God, you have my attention over this one."

Some of the breakups have been of the "Phew!" variety, from my sons' and my point of view, and some have broken our hearts, mother and child both.

A couple of breakups had me wondering if there shouldn't be a law forbidding kids from such an act until after they received permission from their mothers. If so, I would not have granted it because I had fallen in love with this girl who already seemed like my family. Nobody asked me if I was ready for it to end.

When my sons grew older and moved away, they sometimes brought their love interests home to meet the family during holidays. Some of their love interests didn't travel well. No, not well at all. At least that's what the boys told us. They swore that kind of behavior had never been displayed before.

And how do you know when it's time to start buying the current love interest gifts? I began feeling like a jinx when, for the third time in a row, I bought a gift for someone my son was no longer dating by the time the holiday rolled around, and sometimes that was a very short gap. When I decided not to tempt fate in that way, the Ms. Wonderfuls were, of course, still around and showering me with delightful presents that made me feel like a loser because I had nothing with which to reciprocate.

You want to love the significant other because your child does; you don't want to see them plunge headlong into obvious disaster. You don't want to say anything bad about what you perceive to be a horrendous match. Neither do you want to hold your tongue and have them get on Oprah one day, saying they have been estranged from their mothers and in counseling for twenty-five years because Mom never told them the truth. I can read the TV Guide already: *Sons who love psychotic women and whose mothers knew it all along, but didn't tell because they love their sons.*

You want them to chose someone like you because it would be so flattering. On the other hand, you're afraid they'll choose a better version of you, thereby wrecking your self-esteem and making you prime talk show fodder: *Mothers whose sons marry women just like them only better.*

You want them to be happy, even if you believe you might one day need to wear Mother of the Groom Leathers, because that seems to be the outfit of choice for both your son and his current cutie.

Then you finally get tired of trying to read the future, and decide to put it in God's hands. You take to heart the mother who said she began praying for her children's spouses the day her kids were born. In fact, she prayed for the parents of her children's spouses. And you wish you'd done the same.

But you decide to get off that fruitless guilt trip and, with all the spare time you save by not flogging yourself, you undertake redecorating your kitchen. You find yourself choosing this very large and deep sink because you see your fat-cheeked little grandchild sitting down in the basin while you squirt them with the cleverly designed and very costly combination faucet/spray thingie.

I'm sure I had a dreamy glow on my face as I stood like Vanna in front of the vowels showing Brian our new sink and carrying on about his one-day little cherub, whom I pictured as having the best features of his parents and loving his grandmother to pieces.

Not long after telling Brian my dream, I was parting the hair on the side of my head to show him how much silver I was accumulating. (I don't dye my hair; I "color enhance the pigment-impaired parts.")

"I better hurry up with those grandkids!" he said.

"What?"

"I didn't know you were *that* old."

"Please, Brian. How about getting a girlfriend first? Then a wife? Then a child? A billion gray hairs are all I can handle right now."

No, son. Not to hurry. Don't pace your life or change your plans or make your choices on account of me. I mean it. Just think about all the guys I dated...

No son. Don't think about that. I mean it.

And don't pay any attention to the fact that I occasionally whip your photo out of my wallet and show it to someone who has just the right cheekbones and a kind heart and a bright smile and a giving spirit and who is available. Just in case you were looking. Just in case you wanted me to help you. Just in case God needs a hand. Just in case.

50 Batten the Hatches, My Hormones Are on the Loose

I was having lunch with a friend when all of a sudden (and I mean all-of-a-sudden,) she yanked off her blazer and nearly threw it on the floor just to get it away from her.

"Gads, it's hot in here," she gasped, picking up a napkin and fanning herself so quickly that her arm was propelling like the Roadrunner's (beep-beep) legs.

"Do you think it suddenly got hot in here?" I asked.

"Yes."

"Well it didn't. You're having a hot flash," I said, giving that knowing nod of the head as I studied her flushed face.

"No way."

"Way. I've had a few trillion myself."

"But I still get my period."

"I know, but you start getting weird menopause symptoms long before you stop having your period. I've been doing a lot of reading about it. Can't be too informed."

It's true. I have been doing a lot of reading about menopause. Lots of strange things have been happening to me over the last several years, and I discovered that many of them are perimenopausal symptoms. What a relief! I had dreamed up all kinds of ailments. The relief is not in having the annoying and troublesome and sometimes downright scary symptoms, but in learning that I'm okay. That ringing ears and aching joints and near desperate waves of tiredness and incredible mood swings and loss of concentration and on and on *ad nauseam* can all be normal parts of menopause. Normal parts. And I'm having them all.

Mom isn't around anymore to answer these questions that pop into my mind. To tell me what it was like. Although I tried querying other ladies from her generation, mum seems to be the word. They're embarrassed by the question and uncomfortable talking about it. They didn't have time for it. They never noticed anything. It was no problem.

But just ask their families. To say it went unnoticed is absolutely not true.

"Mom was a raging maniac."

"My Aunt started sleeping with a gun under her pillow."

"Her personality simply snapped for several years."

"She was worried she was cracking up."

"She was so crabby I wanted to knock her in the head."

I've even brought the topic up in mixed company. If I can't think of a word or something, I laugh and say, "Menopause." Always they laugh with me. I want society to get used to hearing us casually say the word without fear or shame.

I've talked about this with my boys. I want them to know I'm going through something and to be patient. Just like I was patient with them when their hormones were racing. (Okay, I was patient most of the time.)

The other day I heard a speaker talking about her kids aged two and fifteen. She said they're going through identical phases. They don't want you to expect them to know how to do anything. They don't understand the word "no"; they use it all the time. They're moody; they're excitable.

Yup, I was thinking, *sounds like menopause.*

Not all women encounter symptoms, any symptoms. But many of us do. We need to educate not only us, but people in our Space.

Perhaps most importantly, we need to laugh at ourselves. Come on, wanting to strip buck naked when it's only fifty-five in the conference room is funny. Isn't it? Wanting to punch out the lights of anyone who looks at you cockeyed is a hoot, right? Bloating and sleepless nights and spotting are real side splitters, huh?

Okay, so it's not REALLY funny, but we can learn to find the humor in our situation. For when we don't laugh, when we don't tell our stories, we do a disservice not only to ourselves, but our daughters and their daughters as well.

So how about it? Here's a few ideas to help activate you into becoming more comfortable with this phase of your life:

- Slam this book closed at the end of this chapter and start making Menopause banners that say, "Batten the hatches! My hormones are on the lose."
- Initiate neighborhood Menopause clubs and meet every Wednesday at noon. (Make sure it's a large and well ventilated room lest you all flash at the same time and ignite the place.)
- Use the word *menopause* as your new verb. A few examples: "I could have menopaused all night." "Allow me to menopause with you." "Menopause your way to health, happiness and fulfillment." "Stand back, I'm going to menopause right now!"
- Buy stock in Kleenex then watch it skyrocket as you pur-

chase barge loads to sop up the floods of your crying jags.

- Make Art Deco necklaces out of the empty packets from your estrogen patches.
- Wear an undershirt with a big "M" on it and scurry to the aid of woman in hysterical crisis.
- Begin wearing adult diapers NOW so you can free up all that time you spend in: a) having to go to the bathroom; b) waiting in line to go to the bathroom; c) going to the bathroom; d) changing your underwear.

But whatever you do, do it with style and grace. Do it with abandon and refuse to be embarrassed by your body.

Who knows, maybe you'll relish this transition in your life and hope The Days of Menopause never end.

But I doubt it.

When All Is Said and Done

(which, of course, it never is)

I hope my days have tickled your joy receptors and stirred some warm memories.

But more importantly, I hope you're inspired to tell your stories to someone. What gain does it net us to keep our *faux pas*, and especially our joys, to ourselves?

I can't tell you how many times after I'm done speaking and barely off the stage (as I'm hurtling for the bathroom) that someone will rush up to me, thank me profusely, then go on to say what a relief it was to find they aren't the only one that "stuff like THAT" ever happens to.

They are anxious to tell me their horror and victory stories. I'm anxious to listen and know I am not roaming around the country leaving a wake of stunned and shocked people behind me who don't have a clue WHAT I'm talking (and writing) about. Tattling on yourself releases the pressure valve and primes the pump for others to give sharing a whirl.

Life is to be enjoyed and celebrated, so that even in the midst of the wackiest and most craziest times, we can laugh.

You don't get days back; you can't do them over. So why not make the most of them?

I once read a quote that said, "Every tomorrow has two handles: that of anxiety, and that of enthusiasm. Upon your choice, so will be the day."

Your life is the sum total of your days. Consider the options. After all, you're alive! Give thanks. And remember what Mama said.

A NOTE TO THE READER

This book was selected by the book division of the company that publishes *Guideposts*, a monthly magazine filled with true stories of people's adventures in faith.

If you have found inspiration in this book, we think you'll find monthly help and inspiration in the exciting stories that appear in our magazine.

Guideposts is not sold on the newsstand. It's available by subscription only. And subscribing is easy. All you have to do is write Guideposts, 39 Seminary Hill Road, Carmel, New York 10512. For those with special reading needs, *Guideposts* is published in Big Print, Braille, and Talking Magazine.

When you subscribe, each month you can count on receiving exciting new evidence of God's presence and His abiding love for His people.

Guideposts is also available on the Internet by accessing our homepage on the World Wide Web at http://www.guideposts.org. Send prayer requests to our Monday morning Prayer Fellowship. Read stories from recent issues of our magazines, *Guideposts*, *Angels on Earth*, *Guideposts for Kids* and *Positive Living*, and follow our popular book of daily devotionals, *Daily Guideposts*. Excerpts from some of our best-selling books are also available.